VISION
REALIZED!

VISION REALIZED!

How Top Executives Bridge Vision to Achievements Through Project Management

MOUNIR A. AJAM

Testimonials and Endorsements

Ms. Barbara Carkenord

IIBA Board of Directors and Carkenord Consulting

"Mounir is a thought leader in project management and corporate solutions. He has a deep understanding of how organizations need to manage projects, large and small, to solve problems and continue a successful growth strategy in their market. He analyzes situations carefully and recommends solutions that bring business value."

Mr. Ahmad Y. Alkhiary

Deputy Chairman of Arabian Information Technology Co. (ARCOM)

"When I took my project management course in Khobar, Saudi Arabia, Mounir was the instructor. His deep and comprehensive experience was reflected in class and made it alive. I am grateful to him and wish to take more courses with him."

Mr. Amr Maraie
Project Management Practitioner

"Mounir is the kind of person who always offers revolutionary perspectives on things. He transformed my approach to project management, encouraging a more advanced and critical mindset."

Mr. Mark Moore
Executive Consultant at M2 Project Consulting Corporation

"I've been connected to Mounir Ajam as a "cyber colleague" for many years. Over that span of time, we have interacted many times, and I have found him to be a fantastic source of knowledge and experience, especially when considering large capital projects. Mounir is a creative and collaborative thinker who is always searching for ways to expand his sphere of influence and incorporate other points of view. His writing on project management is in the top tier of what is available today. His global reputation is well-earned, and I am happy to consider him a valued colleague."

Mr. Navaid Jamal

Founder, IMG Advisors LLC

"Mounir is a leader in project management and capital projects. He has a distinctive leadership style that believes in knowledge sharing. As such, he has written books and created opportunities to teach and promote project management.

He is currently pursuing the launch of a comprehensive project management platform, Uruk, that will be used to manage projects with clarity."

Dedication

To the future generations of project executives and managers. Those who dare to explore and travel the rugged roads to reach the beauty of nature and life. Those with the will and determination to break the status quo and aspire for a better future!

CONTENTS

CLOSING

BACK MATTER

Acknowledgment

I want to extend my gratitude to everyone who has supported this project. Your invaluable contributions, through ideas and content reviews, have brought this work to fruition.

First, I want to acknowledge the reviewers and those who offered content, strategy comments, and suggestions, including comments on the various related LinkedIn posts. Your constructive feedback and suggestions have greatly improved the quality of this work. This group includes my executive advisor/coach, Ms. Andrea Nicholas, and colleagues, Mr. Bill Duncan, Mr. Trevor K. Nelson, Ms. Sandra Hoskins, Mr. Mahdi AlKhatib, Mr. Thomas Walenta, Dr. Waffa Adam, Mr. Robert McMartin, Mr. Stephen W. Mass, Mr. Amr Maraie, Mr. Kiron D Bondale, Ms. Becky Winston, Mr. Jean-Charles Savornin, Dr. Ian Heptinstall, and Dr. Mihail Sadeanu. Your insights and feedback have been incredibly helpful.

Further, I want to thank my friend and colleague, Mr. Nah Wee Yang, for illustrating the organizational culture I used in the book.

I am grateful to others who have contributed in various ways, notably in publishing the book. Your efforts have added significant value to this project. This group includes Mr. Steve Gordon and his team.

I also want to thank those who provided testimonies or endorsements. I appreciate your trust and value in our relationship.

Finally, I cannot close this acknowledgment without offering my sincere appreciation to a thought leader whom I highly respect, Mr. Adrian Dooley, who graciously agreed to write the Foreword for this book.

Thank you all for your unwavering support and dedication.

Foreword

Projects and their management have a long history of contributing to the progress of mankind. Of course, for centuries, they weren't recognised as 'projects' and the discipline of project management wasn't formalised. Those in charge simply did what they needed to do to get the job done.

In the mid-20th Century, ideas about how to manage projects became more formalised and documented. Up until that point most projects concerned with 'visible' infrastructure – you could see their end results emerging as the work was done. As we entered the information age, projects became less tangible and much more complex to manage.

Information projects and change projects have quickly become integral to implementing the strategies of public and private organisations. Project management as a discipline needs to adapt to these new demands, as do those who apply it – the 'profession'.

To some extent this adaptation has happened but the effect has been to create divisions and compartments. The battle of Agile vs Waterfall has been disruptive and the current trend to paper over the resulting cracks with 'Hybrid' is not the solution.

While project management has been trying to deal with this rapid technological change, another cultural change has been taking place. Since the 1990s we have seen an inexorable rise in the importance placed on certifications. These mostly focus on learning a narrow range of knowledge with the primary objective of passing an exam and have accelerated the compartmentalization of the discipline and profession.

Numerous pundits cite (often dubious) statistics that demonstrate how the success rate of projects is not improving. Whether or not these statistics are robust, there is no doubt that too many projects fail. The same pundits often propose simple solutions. Of course, there are no quick fixes.

I believe we need to take a deep breath and put fads and fashions behind us. We need something of a reset that will not come from learning project management from social media posts or a multiple-choice exam.

'Back to basics' is an overused, and often abused, term but we do need to get back to the underlying principles and accept that those principles can be adapted to all domains and levels of complexity.

Mounir has a long career and great depth of experience, I believe that books like this will rebuild the edifice of the discipline rather than paper over the cracks. It promotes an holistic view and focuses on what's important.

I believe it will contribute to a reset in the way we regard and practice project management.

Adrian Dooley
Honorary Fellow of the Association for Project Management
Founder of Praxis Framework, https://www.praxisframework.org/
Surrey, United Kingdom.

Preface

The Book Purpose

What is the purpose of this book? Here are the quick answers:

- **Why**: We[1] aim to enable organizations to optimize their capital deployment and deliver excellent shareholder and stakeholder value. It is about enabling and supporting them toward the **Vision Realized!**[2]

  Why

  What

  How

  In business, we often measure value in revenues, profit, return on investment, and other financial metrics. However, in not-for-profit organizations and government work, the value might not be

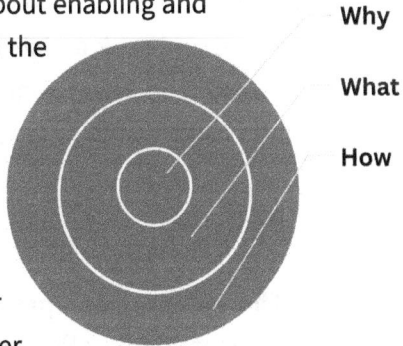

---

[1] Throughout this book, the use of "we" refers to my team at UrukPM or myself (instead of "I"). However, "we" sometimes refers to the collective project management community. Further, we also use "We" to position ourselves as a stakeholder in the transformation that we are proposing. The reader should be able to figure out the proper context.

[2] Unless otherwise noted, we use "vision" to represent vision, mission, values, and purpose.

about commercial gain; instead, we could define it using other variables.[3]

- **What**: Provide these organizations with the mechanism and ability to **achieve impactful strategy implementation** where they do the right projects[4] (e.g., project selection) and deliver value through successful projects and programs (e.g., project performance). In other words, it is vital to ensure that organizations **maintain focus across the entire innovation pipeline and value stream**, from project selection to benefits realizations.

- **How**: We advocate shifting paradigms so that executives do not have to tolerate projects and project management failures and **seek a vision where they can predetermine success**. This would require **understanding, recognizing, and accepting the strategic value of project management**.

Therefore,

"The How" is our proposal to formalize the project management function and establish a centralized project management organizational unit.

Beginning with the end in mind, **Vision Realized** requires effective and impactful strategy implementation.

---

[3] A relevant video: https://youtu.be/ezvZQdCYHTU.

[4] Projects and programs share similarities. Therefore, programs should also be considered when discussing projects.

Impactful Strategy Implementation

Impactful strategy implementation starts by **linking strategy formulation with strategy implementation**, which we can achieve through strategic project management and a portfolio perspective. This partnership is between the project management function, represented by a chief officer, the chief strategy officer, and other executives. This link and partnership are essential, as we explain later.

> ### CHANGE INITIATIVE
>
> We view programs and projects as change initiatives since each is about creating organizational change. The change could be to create a new asset or to improve an existing asset. In this context, an asset could be a facility, a business process, software, or any other product type.
>
> Some practitioners view organizational change as often limited to changing existing processes that impact people and operations, hence the need for formal organizational change management. However, we believe every project or program results in a change. For successful projects, we must consider the change and how to manage it, whether it is minor or massive.

Once an organization defines its portfolio, it uses project management principles and systems to effectively lead the change initiatives to success (see the text box *Change Initiatives).*

Sadly, we realize that project management performance is currently questionable. Many inhibitors to performance exist, and our current state is not where it should be, which is disappointing and might be discouraging. However, despite these issues, competent project management is essential for success. We emphasize that the competence of people and the maturity of the project management systems are vital. Therefore, organizations must transform project management to deliver on strategies and achieve the vision.[5]

Transforming Project Management

We will be direct and straight to the point: **The project management domain has a problem**. On the surface, it is an image problem. However, the image problem is a symptom of profound challenges, failures, and other issues we must identify and understand to resolve. We explain these various issues and challenges in Part A of this book.

PROJECT MANAGEMENT

In the context of this book, unless we are discussing the management of a single project, the term project management refers to the broad sense of the term, which includes the 4PMs (project, program, product delivery, and portfolio management). This is an organization-wide perspective (i.e., organizational project management).

The project management community (individuals, consultants, thought leaders, associations, and vendors) has failed in multiple aspects. We know that many organizations have project management

---

5   We realize that this statement generalizes the need since we believe that many organizations would benefit from transformation.

centers of excellence and do remarkable things. Further, individuals, associations, and organizations offer valuable content, standards, and guides.

On the other hand, many organizations are still struggling. Some have not adopted formal or systematic project management practices. Some do not have any project management systems or methods. Further, it is unfortunate that some organizations have lost trust in project management if they had trust in it to begin with.

The above is true in the private sector, government, and semi-government entities, for small and large organizations, and in all verticals.

Project management is the mechanism for achieving impactful strategy implementation and maximizing shareholders' value. Therefore, we decided to keep this book focused on the strategic aspects at the executive level. This aim also aligns with Uruk Project Management's (UrukPM)[6] purpose, which is:

> **To enable organizations to elevate performance, optimize their capital deployment, and lead projects to maximize shareholders´ and stakeholders´ value.**

We realize that we still need to converge on transforming project management. We will cover it extensively in a follow-up book; it is a massive topic that deserves a separate project.

---

[6] Uruk Project Management is the organization (startup) founded and led by the author, Mounir A. Ajam. UrukPM is developing the world's first integrated digital solution for the management of the 4PMs (project, program, product, and portfolio management).

The Book Scope and Boundaries

The following is a list of conditions we used to author this book. The list will help in understanding the scope and boundaries of this work.

1. We use "organization(s)" to refer to private companies, government entities, non-governmental organizations, or not-for-profit organizations.
2. Similarly, we use the term organizational unit to refer to a unit within the entity, such as a business unit, division, department, or subsidiary.
3. This work assumes that the organization considered for this proposed model is large enough to have formalized organizational units (business units, divisions, departments).
4. The primary goal of this book is what we outlined earlier. However, to achieve this aim, the mechanism is project management. So, we propose to **establish a formally recognized project management function**.
5. A project management **organizational unit** would represent the function (as a formal unit).
6. We are promoting a bold concept that breaks away from what is commonly accepted. Accordingly, take your time to explore before you judge.
7. The idea of transforming project management is related to organizations and project management for organizations. It is not about the individual roles or skills of a specific role.
8. This book touches on project management offices, but it is not about how to set up or manage a PMO; it is much broader and would lead to higher recognition.

9. It is not about adding a Chief Project Officer (CPO) role. A CPO without a system and a formal function is insufficient; we need both.

10. This book is not about agile, waterfall, hybrid, or other specific models. The project management function and unit must offer a generic and adaptive framework.

The Series

When we started working on this book, we determined it could become massive, which is neither practical nor desirable due to the diversity of the audience that must hear this message. Therefore, we converted the book into a series; each is designed for a different audience with a different concentration. However, for maximum benefits, it would be helpful to view them as an integrated approach.

The series' theme is **Transformation: The Future of Work**, changing mindsets and breaking away from using the same thinking that has been mostly ineffective. Project management is at the heart of this transformation, an essential set of skills that would help organizations succeed!

1. The first book, **Vision Realized**, is for an executive-level audience, since organizations must start with the strategic aspects and the founding of a practical project management function. We cannot transform if executives do not proactively take the lead and ownership. Therefore, this book explores various aspects of the current state of practice. Then, we make the case for change and propose an envisioned future. Understanding that this book offers the vision and what must

be done is vital. We leave the working details to the other books in the series.

2. The second book is about **Successful Transformation!** Once an organization accepts the future of work, as we envisioned and proposed, it would need to establish a transformation program team. Therefore, this second book would be a firsthand guide (a playbook) to help organizations build a sustainable and effective project management function, including the project management unit and organizational project management system, methods, and governance. Accordingly, the audience of this book would be the team that would lead the transformation initiative along with the sponsoring executives.

3. The first two books are essential for the strategic aspects. The third and final book in the series is to shift the focus to the several topics that require change on the journey to **Transforming Project Management**. This compendium includes topics on methodology, success, certifications, cost, schedule, risk, change, communication, and leadership and competency development. Therefore, this book is also for the team leading the transformation initiative. However, it is also valuable to all project management practitioners.

With this trilogy, we would have addressed this vital topic at the executive, management, and project levels. This is essential for a sustainable transformation!

This Book

Excluding the introduction and closing chapters, the book has two primary parts.

- Part A is dedicated to presenting the current state of practice;
- Part B focuses on envisioning the future and the proposed solution.

INTRODUCTION

CHAPTER 1

Mindsets and Alternative Reality

An Executive Nightmare

In the dead of night, George was trapped in a relentless project review session. The room was stifling, and beads of sweat trickled down his forehead as he faced a sea of red on the presentation slides. Each red mark symbolized a critical issue, a missed deadline, or a budget overrun. The weight of the problems bore down on him, amplifying his anxiety. His heart raced as he struggled to find solutions, but the red marks only seemed to multiply, engulfing most of the screen. The nightmare felt all too real, a stark reminder of the immense pressure and responsibility that came with his role.

Most projects during the review had one or more problems that could affect shareholders' value or miss a customer critical delivery date. Some projects even faced the potential of total failure or missing most, if not all, of their vital objectives.

George woke up drenched in sweat. A day is ruined!

Have you faced such situations in real life?

We have.

We remember meetings where the actual project expenditure exceeded the forecasted cost.

We remember when some project managers could not tell us when to expect project completion or the final cost.

Every project review session became like a losing battle and led to arguments.

Maybe you did not have nightmares, but you had pain points that caused the occasional sleepless night.

As executives, we have a choice: tolerate the pain or do something about it. This book helps with the latter choice.

An Executive Dream

Catherine is tossing and turning as she dreams. She and other executives are seated around the conference table, surrounded by their teams during the monthly projects' review session. The room is filled with a mix of anticipation and determination.

As the reports are presented, a few projects flash red, signaling challenges that need immediate attention. However, most projects are marked green, showcasing steady progress and successful milestones. Catherine feels a sense of pride and optimism, knowing that, despite the hurdles, the team is on the right track and working cohesively towards its goals. Her husband even hears her sleep talking about her pride in her teams.

When she woke up, Catherine reflected on her dream. She knew that the mental image of the review session was not their reality today due to the various pain points they were experiencing. However, she saw the possibilities and a vision of a bright future.[7]

Waking Up To Reality

Whether you are having nightmares, losing sleep, or having pleasant dreams, the alternative reality can become a reality. Recognizing the problems, challenges, and opportunities can open the door to the hidden potential (Grant, 2023) that exists within each individual and organization. Even if you are doing well, becoming better may be a possibility.

It might be time to rethink (Grant, 2021) our practices, challenge our conventional thinking, and explore our hidden potential so we can nurture and build a great future.

Success is possible.[8] However, we must work to achieve it!

Can We Predetermine Success?

PROJECTS DELIVER VALUE WHEN SUCCESS IS PREDETERMINED, CULTIVATED, AND ACHIEVED

---

[7] In total transparency, we used Microsoft Co-Pilot to write The Nightmare and The Dream. We provided the prompt and edited the results.

[8] A relevant video: https://youtu.be/wQrl9HvV1Xs

Well,

It depends on how you understand "predetermine."

Some view it as a guarantee. In that case, we cannot predetermine success since no one can guarantee it.

However, we use this word to **stress the need for executives and project teams to proactively think of success consciously and consistently instead of wishing or hoping for success**. When we wish or hope for success, we might accept failure or less-than-optimal performance and settle for completion as success. **We want to change the paradigm from tolerating failure to achieving success, which starts with our intentional predetermination.**

Therefore, predetermining success consists of three vital steps:

1. Establishing **a solid business case** for the change initiative (project, program, or transformation).
2. A sound business case is insufficient. The organization must conduct **a proper feasibility study**. A feasibility study helps an organization decide if it can successfully deliver the change initiative and realize the expected benefits. If in doubt, the project should be stopped or reconsidered.
3. Management decided to move forward; what is next? They must define the success criteria. Without well-defined and quantitative (where possible) criteria, success is subjective to opinion-based assessment. The Uruk Way Four Dimensions of Project Success[9] recommends **setting up the criteria for all four dimensions early in the project**.

---

[9]   Refer to Chapter 13 for an elaboration on the Four Dimensions of Project Success.

The Hidden Battle

Before we close this chapter, we want to reflect on the tension in our professional and business community. It is vital to understand this hidden battle mindset. It is at the core of the current state of practice and one of the primary triggers for the envisioned future we propose in this book.

We often hear or read about project management offices (PMOs) needing to continue proving value to executives. We hear PMO directors fighting or wondering why they do not have a seat at the table (i.e., the executives' table and decision-making). Project managers complain about not getting enough support or sponsorship. Yet our community accepts positioning ourselves (PMOs) as service providers and support functions, not as an integral part of the organization. Further, we often see an artificial separation between PMOs and project delivery (or project management in general). They are becoming like separate domains. Reality tells us that, for these reasons and many others, we often see more failures than successes.

Shifting our attention to executives, we notice the following: a few executives might see project management as a transactional or operational domain, and what exists is okay, i.e., there is no need for change. Some executives discuss the need for project management but do not see how to achieve success; there is too much noise and confusion in the community. Some believe project management is critical but lacks a clear, impactful path. Others see delays, problems, budget overruns, quality issues, and nightmares, so they question the value. Consequently, some executives lose trust in project management and their PMOs (if they have one), and some go as far as questioning the need for projects or project management. Consequently, they are waiting for their PMOs to prove their value.

What a dilemma.

How can we break from this reality?

CHAPTER 2

Executive Summary

Challenges and Failures

Project and Project Management

Numerous surveys, studies, and books have documented project management failures, represented by project delays, budget overruns, and even project failures (*see text box titled Project versus Project Management*). Depending on the reference, we have seen reports claiming that only 0.5% of projects achieved their cost, time, and business goals (Flyvbjerg & Gardner, 2023). A 2014 PwC report claims that only *"2.5% of companies successfully completed 100% of their projects"* (PwC, 2014). Other reports claim that 70% of projects fail[10], while in capital projects, we have seen studies that show that 60% are successful (Barshop, 2016). Even the success rate of megaprojects (those costing more than one billion dollars) is 35% or lower (Merrow, 2011).

Consequently, the reality, backed up by studies and surveys from various organizations, shows that we have more failures than

---

[10] This is a common claim that is frequently used in online posts; however, it has been challenged due to lack of evidence or context.

successes. Why do projects fail despite years of professionalism in project management, millions of certificate holders, hundreds or thousands of books and software tools, and many certifications from various associations?

PROJECT VERSUS PROJECT MANAGEMENT

Please note that we differentiate between project management success-failure and project success-failure. The distinction is necessary since a project could face cost and schedule problems but still meet its primary goals.

For example, a café project might still deliver value, revenue, and profit, even if it costs more than the budget and finishes behind schedule.

The opposite could also be true; a project could have excellent cost and schedule performance but not deliver its expected benefits. This could happen if the business case or feasibility studies were faulty or for other unforeseen reasons.

Therefore, when we say, "yet projects continue to fail," it could be project or management failure.

> *Why do projects fail despite years of professionalism in project management?*

The consequences of projects and project management failures for organizations are billions of dollars (if not trillions) in losses or lost opportunities. Failure of critical projects can even threaten the entire business.

Why Do Projects Fail?

Today, many believe that project management is widely spread and accepted, *yet projects continue to fail.*

Numerous software tools are branded as "project management software." These are tools for task management, timesheet management, collaborations, and other functionalities. *Despite all these tools, projects continue to fail.*

Further, we have many guides from project management associations and international standardization committees, *yet projects continue to fail.*

We also have hundreds of certifications and millions of certification holders, *yet projects continue to fail.*

So, why do projects fail?

A quick answer, which might be controversial, is that we (as a community) have not found and addressed the root causes. We are often distracted or get lost in the symptoms. For example, we do not have a standard definition of success and how to assess it, leading to endless debates due to the lack of common ground. In other words, we do not have a baseline, a reference that we can agree on, and in the absence of a reference, how can we measure progress or growth?

If we shift the discussion outside the direct influence of project management, we realize that organizations do not typically face problems in formulating strategy and the organization's strategic direction. However, they often face strategy implementation[11] failures. Consequently, **they fail to bridge the gap between the formulated strategy and achieving the desired outcomes.** Therefore, we must start with an organizational strategic plan and the executives behind it to transform project management and achieve impactful results.

What Is The Root Cause?

If we ask five people why projects fail, we will likely get 50 "causes." We will hear about change, scope creep, lack of clarity on requirements, market conditions, teams' or contractors' performance, materials delivery, the weather, methodology, etc. The symptoms might vary depending on a project's industry, type, size, or complexity. However, we believe most of those reasons are system failure symptoms.

If we drill down, one "root cause" might seem to be the lack of focus on the entire project value stream. Another apparent root cause might be the absence of organizational project management systems and methods. One more possibility is the lack of transparent and effective project governance. One more potential cause might be the lack of proper planning or framing. These ideas are close to the root cause, but not yet.

> *We hypothesize that the root cause starts with the lack of recognition of project management as a core organizational function; everything else is a symptom or a side effect.*

---

[11]   It is common to use implementation and execution interchangeably.

We hear a lot about the "Project Economy" and the importance of project management. We might hear other ideas about project management value contradicting our statement on the lack of recognition. We think we have fallen into the knowing-doing gap (Pfeffer & Sutton, 1999). We might talk big, but our actions do not align or rise to the needed responsibility and accountability level. Hence, the need for this book.

Are We Not Improving?

For decades, despite the growth in members of professional associations, certifications, certification holders, and many software, books, etc., we have not seen any meaningful change in projects' performance. At best, we have seen fluctuations in the rate of success. However, **project management failures are still too common**, if not dominant. **Our collective work has not compensated for the confusion and fragmentation of project management**. We are not learning from our history; it is like treating a significant injury with a band-aid.

> *It is time to break away from our past and seek what might appear to be radical change.*

This book is our attempt to break the cycle of doom. We will present the current reality and the case for change, offer our solution, and then offer the mechanism to build the future before closing with practical tips.

The Proposed Solution

Introduction

In 2007, we started a project management innovation (research and development program) to improve project management practice, which led to the Uruk Way.[12] We[13] also studied the challenges associated with project management offices. Since then, we have published a few books, but none have focused on transforming project management or revolutionizing the PMO practice. In the summer of 2024, **we decided it was time to tackle this topic since, for close to two decades, we have not seen any notable change in project success despite the growth in terms of guides, certifications, software, and certified individuals.**

Accordingly, this book proposes a solution as the starting point for achieving impactful strategy implementation and transforming the project management state of practice.

What is this solution, and how can we achieve it?

First, we must stress that this proposal is for the organization's executive management and board of directors. They are the only ones that have the power to act and lead!

---

[12] The SUKAD Way Project Management Framework, rebranded as The Uruk Framework: https://urukpm.com/the-uruk-way-project-management/.

[13] At that time, the effort was primarily made by Mounir A. Ajam and Luc Bauwmans (professor at Central Queensland University now).

Second, it should be evident that this proposal is for organizations large enough to have formal divisions or departments and that they do deliver value through projects.

The Solution

The solution could have many elements, but we must start with two integrated parts:

1. **Building and sustaining an effective and practical project management function** (PMF): a PMF is much broader than the flavors of PMO[14] we have experienced in our community. A PMF is a core organizational function, not a service provider.[15] Accordingly, a strategic PMF requires formal organizational recognition and acceptance. The mandate of a PMF (and its related organizational unit) includes linking strategy formulation with implementation, building the organizational project management system (OPMS), and leading the 4PMs (Integrated Delivery).[16]

2. **Integration to Deliver Value** is crucial for establishing the PMF and developing the OPMS. This includes "vertical" and "horizontal" integrations. Vertical integration is related to linking the 4PMs;[17] horizontal integration is a model like the Value Delivery Methodology (VDM). The VDM focuses on value delivery from project ideation to initial operations. This would be done by following a well-defined methodological

---

14 One way to think of it as sanctioned turbo-charged PMO!
15 A relevant video: https://youtu.be/TF1Da6dXurl.
16 This is the focus of Part B and, most specifically, Chapters 9 and 10.
17 4PMs = Project, Program, Product, and Portfolio Management.

process that respects the diversity of our practice through adaptive standards (tailoring).[18]

What Is The Outcome?

Emphasizing what we shared earlier, we aim to help organizations[19] realize their vision and maximize shareholders' and stakeholders' value by optimizing performance and implementing impactful strategies. **Our purpose is to elevate competence and performance.**

Organizational success depends on many factors, but one vital area is linked to the performance of the portfolio of projects.[20] Accordingly, we must transform project management to optimize performance since it is the mechanism and the engine of project success.

In this case, the outcome results from a higher success rate of the various change initiatives and the entire portfolio, which leads to value creation. We recognize that organizations can achieve excellent value from their operations and innovation. However, our book focuses on project management as the engine to achieve the outcome of change initiatives and innovation. In other words, **successful innovation is an outcome of projects and programs.**

Reflecting on what we already mentioned, despite the advancement of technology, software tools, various professional associations, and millions of professionals with one or more certifications, we do not see a notable change in performance. Therefore, we know that we

---

[18]   This is the focus of Part B and, most specifically, Chapters 11 to 13.

[19]   In this context, "organizations" refer to companies (small and large), government entities, non-governmental organizations, and not-for-profit organizations.

[20]   A relevant video (Novel Perspectives on Project Success): https://youtu.be/wQrl9HvV1Xs.

must transform project management. Please reflect on the Hidden Battles from Chapter 1.

Change initiatives and transformation can follow different paths. The two most common paths are:

- **Bottom-up**: which can be authentic and grassroots but slow in influencing upward.

- **Top down**: the fastest and most effective, if genuine.

Our proposed solution must pursue both paths to be most effective. The outcome is a project management function that can enable impactful strategy implementation.

Project Management Maturity

Project management maturity (PMM) is an important topic that requires much more than we share here. We limit the discussion to emphasize the importance of PMM and its relation to project performance and success.

Therefore, before we explain the benefits and share studies, it is essential to explain a vital concept: project management maturity. PMM, also known as Organizational Project Management Maturity (OPMM), describes the level of maturity of the project management practice within an organization. PMM starts with standardizing the processes (policies, guides, methods, governance) and requires the various project management teams to follow the system.

It is worth noting that there is no standard maturity model in project management. Various models exist, like the Berkely Model we mention here. However, most models share a common concept: assessment models with scores from 1 to 5, with 1 being the lowest level. Some practitioners use Level 0 to show the absence of any project management formality within an organization. Other models do not use this scoring approach.

The first image is from the University of California Berkeley, Business Process Management Office.[21] This model is not limited to project management, but it is representative of maturity models.

It is important to note that organizations perform significantly better with a higher level of maturity. Here is a direct quotation from the Business Process Management Office at UC Berkeley.[22]

> *"The scale has 5 incremental levels where each level builds on the governance, ownership, documented processes, and performance metrics. **As you grow in Process Maturity, you increase your ability to navigate change, realize project benefits, and increase adoption and usage.**"*

---

[21] https://bpm.berkeley.edu/process-architecture/process-maturity.
[22] The same as the previous note.

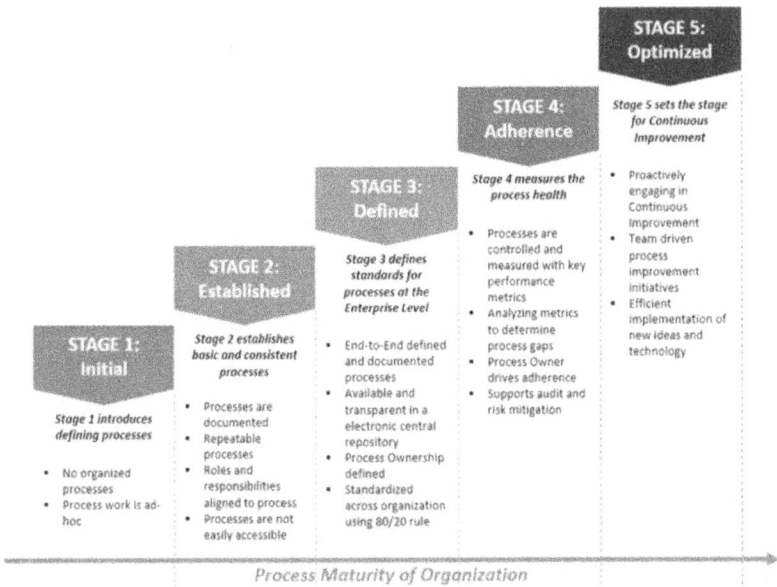

Figure No 2.1: University of California Berkeley, Process Management - Maturity

The Benefits

Studies – Performance

Numerous studies, including those by the University of California Berkeley (Ibbs & Reginato, 2002), Independent Project Analysis (Barshop, 2016), professional associations, and others have demonstrated that organizations with higher levels of project management maturity (including the use of proper methodological processes) can achieve significant benefits. The benefits include:

- With the proper methodological process,[23] organizations can achieve a significant increase in speed to market, up to 30%,

---

[23] A methodological process is part of project management maturity (would start with stage 2 but should be stable by stage 3).

and are 2.5x more likely to be on budget and on time (Stage Gate International, 2024).

- Independent Project Analysis benchmarking data show that following the proper methodological process[24] could lead to a 5% increase in the expected Net Present Value (NPV) versus a reduction of up to 45% if no method is followed (Barshop, 2016).

The next illustration is also from the University of California Berkeley[25] (UCB). However, this is from a study that links the organization's project management maturity with project performance (Ibbs & Reginato, 2000). This study is specific to project management. However, comparing the two images, you can notice the five stages.[26]

A concise explanation of the study producing the shared illustration gives us two vital findings:

1. With increased project management maturity, project performance (cost and schedule) significantly improves (the X-axis), and

2. The cost of managing projects in the organization will decrease once the organization achieves Stage 3 (the line).

We do not include the other benefits identified in the Berkeley study here to keep the focus on the critical points.

---

[24] This includes a project life cycle/stage gate model (a methodological process).

[25] The author is a UCB 1990 graduate with a master's degree in civil engineering, specializing in Engineering and Project Management.

[26] We often use stages, steps, and levels interchangeably.

Scenario 1

The impact of project management maturity on project performance

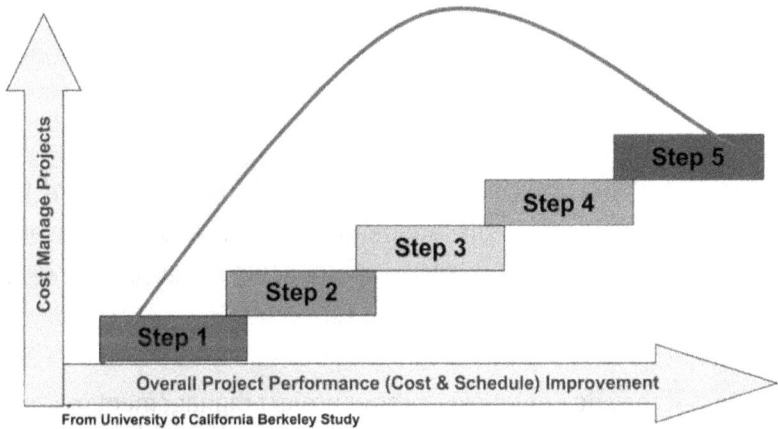

Figure No 2.2: The Impact of Project Management Maturity on Project Performance

Quantifying the Benefits

Let us discuss a hypothetical scenario.

Imagine an organization with US$10 million in annual project spending. Also, assume 10% cost savings (up to 20% is possible). Even if we ignore time savings or opportunities gained from speed to market, the benefit is $1 million.

Further, many organizations working on capital-intensive projects (facilities) could have a capital program worth $100 million,[27] and

---

[27] An operating facility (industrial, utility, power) could have an annual capital program of $50 to 100 million. This budget level would be for maintaining capacity or upgrading projects. In comparison, the same company could have a budget of a few billion dollars when it includes its new, large, complex, or mega projects.

some have budgets of billions of dollars. Can you imagine the savings and opportunities gained from faster market entry and cost reduction? On one megaproject we worked on, the opportunity gain was $1M+ per day!

Scenario 2

Here is another example that demonstrates the finding of the benchmarking study by the Independent Project Analysis (Barshop, 2016). A project is expected to generate $10M in net present value (NPV).[28]

- If they do not follow a proper project management method, the project NPV can experience up to 45% reduction, i.e., the actual NPV would drop to $5.5 million ($4.5 million reduction).
- If the same project follows an effective method, it could achieve a 5% increase in NPV, or $10.5 million.
- The 5% might seem low, but we should compare $10.5 to $5.5 million. The $5M difference is vast.

An Exercise

Here is a quick exercise for you:

- Figure out your annual capital budget,
- Find the anticipated NPV for these projects,
- Calculate your potential impact (gain).
- If you think the 45% reduction is too high, try with 30%, 20%, or 10%.

---

[28] Most capital projects' NPV would be much, much higher than $10M.

What Are The Consequences Of No Action?

If you did not complete the exercise for the benefits, do it for the consequences.

In total transparency, **the system we propose is non-conventional. We are unaware whether it exists (in its entirety) in today's environment or anywhere in the world, although it could. However, we know that many organizations have pieces of what we propose.** They might have a PMO, a PM Department, a PM System, a methodological process, or something similar. We know of a few organizations in oil and gas that have something close to what we propose. We also know that some service providers and consultant companies might have projectized[29] some of the work, especially for clients' projects.

On the other hand, here is what we know. As we outlined, those organizations with higher project management maturity deliver and improve shareholders' value. They view project management as a strategic set of skills and a competitive advantage.

So,

- If your organization has high maturity and delivers consistent success, you have likely arrived or are close to our proposed destination. However, if you implement this initiative, would you be able to increase the rate of success and achieve further improvement?

---

[29] Projectized is a term in the community that refers to an organization that has adopted a project-led approach for their work.

- On the other hand, if your organization experiences frequent delays in delivering products to market and completing projects and encounters frequent cost and schedule challenges, can you afford to continue experiencing these problems?
- If you belong to an organization that is only achieving 0.5% success on cost, schedule, and overall objectives (Flyvbjerg & Gardner, 2023) can you even survive?

Now, imagine the losses or opportunity losses.

Here are a few massive cases:

- "Kmart's failure was also due to a series of management blunders and poor strategic planning" (IT difficulties help take Kmart down, 2002).
- On one mega project, they experienced a 9-month delay with a $1M/day in opportunity loss (confidential). That is $270 million.
- A Levi Strauss case study where IT projects almost killed this company (Why a botched IT Project will destroy a major corporation in the near future, 2013).
- A recent case study is about a $10B pharmaceutical project and the attempt to rescue it from failure.[30]
- Other famous large-scale projects could include the Euro Tunnel, the Sydney Opera House, The Berlin-Brandenburg Airport Project, and the Boston Big Dig Project.
- Here is a link to a study on government IT projects https://www.belfercenter.org/publication/government-tech-proj-

---

[30] https://www.linkedin.com/pulse/rescuing-10b-pharmaceutical-project-from-failure-micah-piippo-byodc/

ects-fail-default-it-doesnt-have-be-way. It mentions that government tech projects over $6 million only succeed 13% of the time (Lerner, 2020).

Closing Comment

DRYING A WET TOWEL

Let us visualize this scenario: you want to dry a wet towel quickly. Here are some options:

You shake the towel, which removes the excess water but will still be wet.

You wring the towel with your hands as hard as possible. However, the towel will remain wet or inhibit moisture.

An alternative would be to hang it to dry, which will work but takes a long time.

If you can hang it outside where there might be sun, it will dry faster but still take time.

The solution for quick drying might be using a dryer if you have access to one.

This chapter is an executive summary of the book. We will expand on the current state in Part A and then offer the solution in Part B. You will learn actions that start a vital transformation for strategic success within your organization.

Please refer to the text box and consider the following:

The same things (although much more complex than drying a towel) are happening with project management. For example, organizations have tried certifications, generic training, and implementing PMOs without authority or power. Many have tried to blame methodologies, such as traditional, waterfall, and even agile. All these actions led to some improvements. However, organizations were still facing problems.

Consider another example: a car that does not work. We cannot assume or guess the problem. We must examine the various parts of the system. It could be fuel, electricity, an engine issue, or a combination of problems.

These examples lead us to consider alternatives and change our practices (the wet towel). We also need new thinking—system thinking (the car trouble).

Here are a few points to consider before moving on.

- It is vital to align the organization's executives and board of directors with a practical project management function to maximize shareholders' value. Project management is indispensable for success.
- Organizations need a project management function equipped to enhance competence and consistently elevate performance.
- The project management function is a partner for sound strategy formulation and implementation.

We provide a model to envision a future, realize your vision, and bridge vision to achievements through project management.

PART A

The Current State

Introduction to Part A

This part of the book covers the current state of practice to make the case for change.

We subdivided this topic into several chapters to address the current state from various perspectives and components since understanding the entire system is vital (*refer to the text box*).

- Chapter 3, **Inhibitors to Project Performance.** Based on three decades of worldwide experience with many organizations and all types of projects, we discuss several factors that inhibit the performance of projects and change initiatives. **These performance inhibitors significantly affect the ability to achieve success and realize the anticipated benefits of these projects, leading to extensive waste.**

- Chapter 4, **Project Management**: Although the current state of practice in the project management domain is related to performance inhibitors, we decided to cover this topic separately. This chapter addresses many challenges facing the project management community that often lead to confusion, faulty promotions, ethically questionable practices, and even chaos. **We need to guide executives through this chaos.**

SYSTEM THINKING

The project management field's fragmentation is one challenge affecting projects' success and failure. Another related challenge is the separation between the project function and the rest of the organizational functions. These will be obvious as we continue through this and the next part of this book.

Therefore, it is essential to follow the concept of system thinking, i.e., thinking of the various components and alternatives. This is necessary when we discuss the current state and the envisioned future. Organizations that do not fix the entire system might face repeated problems or lower performance.

- Chapter 5, **Project Management Office**: Here, we focus on the current state of practice of project management offices and the evolving ideas of PMOs. Concerning PMOs, we have seen a good deal of success and some highly effective PMOs. On the other hand, we still see confusion, chaos, and failure. **Over a few decades, we have seen the factors that lead to success and the conditions causing failure.**

- Chapter 6, **Project Management in Industries**: We often consider project management a uniform set of processes and ignore our diversity. This relevant discussion highlights the differences and performance within the most popular domains that use project management. **The primary focus of this chapter is to show that we can learn from each other despite the differences and diversity of practice.**

We have been fortunate to spend about 15 years working on capital projects, another 15 in management consultancy and training, and now five years in direct technology leadership. We have worked with conglomerates and led a technology startup. Therefore, we have seen and lived through this diversity.

- Chapter 7, **Project Management and the C-Suite**: This book aims to maximize shareholders' value, which requires impactful strategy implementation enabled by strategic project management. Therefore, discussing the C-Suite view of project management and its recognition or lack thereof is essential. We want to stress that executives cannot continue to "pass the buck" to PMOs and project managers. **Executives are vital in leading, sponsoring, and guiding their organizations' projects. Top executives accept accountability to bridge vision to achievements.**

CHAPTER 3

Inhibitors To Project Performance

Introduction

There are many challenges and reasons for project failure. We found a few leading performance inhibitors in our search for the root cause. In other words, these inhibitors are the topics leading to the root cause of why organizations do not do as well as they could in managing their organizational projects, products, and change initiatives.

First, we must stress that we are not discussing the causes of a project's failure. This is not about a single project; it is about the organization's performance. In other words, what factors limit an organization's ability to perform better? The idea is not about perfection and is independent of the starting point. It is about becoming better with every cycle.

The five primary inhibitors are:

1. Divergent opinions,
2. Lack of organizational acceptance,
3. Organizational divides,

4. Absence of organizational project management, and
5. Confusion about project management methods.

Divergent Opinions

When we explore the project management community about topics such as methodology, technology, project success, and other concepts, we will find diverse opinions. Some are on point, others are misunderstandings, and a few could be bad or misleading, consciously or subconsciously. One part of the problem is often the debates, especially those that push one idea over another without support, context, or clarification.

The consequence of these divergent opinions[31] is the endless debates resulting in confusion and contributing to the poor image. Here are some examples (unfortunately, it is a lengthy list):

1. To promote a good concept, like agile development, some practitioners do not promote it on its merits; they create a villain (waterfall). Then, everything that is good must be agile, and anything wrong must be a waterfall.
2. Similarly, we might find it easier to blame a method rather than take on the responsibility for our actions. Interestingly, some who blame "waterfall" for promoting "agile" now claim agile does not work. Some say, "We need Agile 2.0" or "extreme agile," while others say, "We need Hybrid." A few recent posts even claim that Agile is dead.
3. Staying with Agile, the Agile Manifesto (Manifesto for Agile Software Development, n.d.) presented us with values and

---

[31] We do not have issues with differences of opinion; they are natural and healthy. Our issues are with misleading and unsubstantiated claims.

principles, using a format like this: *"Although we need things from the left and right, we prefer the things on the left."* In practice, some practitioners started to think that we only need the things on the left, and so the items on the right must be wrong.[32]

4. Some[33] do not believe in the value of project management (or have lost trust in it). Also, some think project management is another layer of management (implying bureaucracy).

5. Many believe project management is "common sense" and anyone can manage projects, leading to accidental project manager syndrome[34] (Ajam, Project Management for the Accidental Project Manager, 2013).

Can you say this fast? It is common sense not to depend on common sense on non-common-sense projects!

6. Similarly, some believe project life cycle management (stage gate model) is a bureaucratic process. Also, it would slow down the work due to slow decisions and the various stage gates.

A counterpoint Stage Gate International claims that a stage gate model can increase speed to market by up to 30% (Stage Gate International, 2024)

---

[32] Here is an example: "Working software over comprehensive documentation." The perception was that we do not need documentation.

[33] Professionals, managers, and executives.

[34] We expand on the accidental project manager syndrome in Chapter 7.

7. A few might believe that project management kills innovation.[35]
8. Some want to embrace project management but hear about PMO failures, so they hesitate.

The list can go on.

Further, let us address three other reasons that might not be politically correct. In some situations (maybe a few cases), management might know the value but not implement a system because:

1. Effective project management can expose inefficiencies in the management and individuals.
2. Effective project management can expose incompetence.
3. They know proper project management requires governance, which can expose corruption.

Lack of Organizational Acceptance

Another performance inhibitor is the lack of organizational acceptance.

Many organizations and their executive teams have not yet recognized the value of project management. Even when organizations have moved from no project management processes toward a PMO, we often hear PMO managers and directors complaining about the need to continue proving their value, lack of executive support, and other complaints.

---

[35] Here is a case study from a mega project on this point: https://urukpm.com/case-studies/.

In many (if not most) non-industrial organizations, executives have not reached the mindset that accepts project management as an independent domain.[36] It is a domain that should not be left to accidental project managers.[37] These executives have not recognized project management as an organizational function. A formal function equals marketing, human resources, information technology, finance, and other functions. This is one of the reasons we do not see project management departments or divisions in companies and government organizations.

Here is a question for you:

Does project management exist in your organization as a formal department (or division) like human resources, information technology, or finance? *A PMO (in most cases) is NOT a formal department.[38]*

If there is "some formality," we see a diluted version called PMO, Agile PMO, Next Generation PMO,[39] and many other names of "offices" that may exist for 2 to 3 years. Consequently, organizations do not achieve optimal project performance.

---

[36] A relevant article: https://urukpm.com/rethink-the-project-management-function/

[37] We are not against the idea of an accidental project manager; most of us started our careers as accidental project managers. However, we cannot depend on this alone, and it should be structured. Here is an article on this subject: https://bookboon.com/en/project-management-ebook.

[38] We realize that there we might find some exceptions where a PMO is truly a department equal to other departments.

[39] Chapter 5 covers the current state of the PMO practice.

Organizational Divides

The current trends and hype about Agile and Hybrid show the divide in organizations between "business" and "IT" or product development. When we hear about Agile Project Management and IT Projects, these are clear examples of organizations not being able to see projects as business initiatives, investments, or change initiatives. Instead, they see them in pieces. Each piece is led by a different party, separated by virtual fences or silos.

These organizations do not view these "projects" as business or change initiatives, which must be managed end-to-end across an entire project life cycle, from ideation to operation.

Consequently, when we hear Agile Transformation, we expect[40] to hear the future screams that, like generic certifications, "Agile Project Management" did not deliver the value promised because there is no "Agile Project Management." So, Agile did not work. Let us go back to the waterfall, but we cannot then invent a Hybrid.

The main issue here is not limited to Agile or Hybrid and whether they are project management methods. The challenges related to this performance inhibitor include fragmentation of project management, separation between product and project management, and even isolation of project management from the rest of the business.

---

[40] We initially wrote these words about around 2013 or 2014. So, back to the future, that expectation is here. We have now read about Agile failure and are going to Agile 2.0 or Hybrid.

Think about this: no "technology" or "construction" projects exist. This statement is true if you work in a project owner organization (not a vendor working for a client).

How could that be?

What we often call technology or construction projects are most likely business projects with technology or construction components. In other words, we do not construct buildings for the sake of construction or develop software tools for software development. We do these things to drive business value. However, because of fragmentation and organizational divides, we tend not to see these business initiatives as projects until they reach the IT department or move into the construction stage.

Absence of Organizational Project Management

The next performance inhibitor is the lack of organizational systems to support building project management functions, and the methodological approach used to treat projects as change initiatives. The organizational project management system is about the proper governance, policies, processes, and overall framework for managing the organization's portfolio, including projects and programs.

Along with this system, or its absence, there is a lack of organizational knowledge, history, and lessons learned, which causes the organization to waste much time for no reason with almost every project, not learning the lessons.

Here are a few questions on this point (try to answer them with minimal research):

1. Do you know how many projects are active in your organization now?
2. Do you have records of the projects completed in the last five years?
3. How about the percentage of projects completed within the cost and schedule parameters?
4. Do you have an operating plan that includes all planned projects for the upcoming year? If you do, does it give you information about the level of resources you have or need?
5. Are you capturing lessons learned, and if you are, do you systematically use them to avoid repeating the errors on future projects?
6. Do you measure project success, and what percentage of projects were successful?
7. We can ask many other questions about risk management, change management, scope creep, etc. However, we think you have enough to understand this performance inhibitor.

Confusion About Project Management Methods

The last performance inhibitor might seem focused on software, but it is a broader issue. It is primarily about what constitutes a project management method.[41]

---

[41] On the YouTube Applied Project Management Channel by UrukPM, we have many videos on project management methodology (this is one of them: https://youtu.be/ SiUkQrHQAHY). This was also a core topic in my 2017 book, Project Management Beyond Waterfall and Agile (https://urukpm.com/books/).

There are hundreds of software products mislabeled as "project management software." Most of what exists is for timesheets, some team collaborations, task management, cost or schedule development, etc. These tools would be available for a project manager, assuming the project manager is experienced and knows how to use them. We have seen project personnel use MS Project as a to-do list because they do not know how to schedule.

On the other hand, major organizations could invest millions to custom-build a project management product (software). However, many do not, and many small, medium, and even large organizations do not have a proper project management system. Further, even if they do, it could be basic and not highly effective.

To our knowledge, no methodology-driven software products in the market guide a project manager or organization in successfully leading a project from concept to success. Therefore, this leads to situations where there is nothing and the business of recreating the wheel or spending millions to build the same thing that others might have built.

Moving beyond software, we often read debates or posts about "what the best methodology to use," "Here is a list of project management methodologies," etc. The problem is that what is often listed are not project management methods.[42] They might be guides (e.g., PMBOK® Guide), techniques (e.g., earned value management), development approaches (e.g., agile, waterfall, iterative, incremental), and other confusions. The root cause of this confusion is that many

---

[42] We often interchange the terms method and methodology, which might be okay in some contexts. However, they are different. Here is a video about the differences: https://youtu.be/S817gxN6TuY.

in the community cannot distinguish between project work (e.g., product development, engineering, construction, web design) and project management (e.g., estimating, scheduling, risk, and change management). They confuse the process groups (PMI® and ISO®) with project phases.

This can be a lengthy topic, but we said enough. The vital point to stress is this: if we in the project management community cannot agree on fundamental concepts, why should executives trust us?

Closing Remarks

In summary, what we see is:

- Organizations should transform their culture and mindset and move toward building their project management functions, including the proper organizational structure and recognition.
- The need to go beyond the hype and what is popular. Therefore, they need to address what is needed and essential for success. What is essential is managing projects end to end by breaking the organizational barriers and silos.
- There is a lack of well-defined, proper, and sustainable organizational project management systems with the right processes and knowledge base.
- The absence of accessible and comprehensive methodology-centric online software solutions.

We will elaborate more in later chapters.

CHAPTER 4

Project Management

Introduction

We start with a disclaimer.

When we discuss the high project failure rate, we cannot generalize that this is the case everywhere. On the contrary, we have seen outstanding performances. Also, remember that we are likely discussing project management failures and successes in many of these situations rather than the overall project objectives.

- In one organization, the goal was that at least 90% of the projects must be successful, and cost success was defined as +/- 10% of the budget, and they achieved it year after year. Therefore, we know success is possible.
- Benchmarking information from the Independent Project Analysis (IPA) of capital projects, as documented in the book Capital Projects by Paul Barshop, showed us that the success rate was about 60% (Barshop, 2016). These were projects in

the millions (many were over $100 million) of US dollars but not megaprojects.[43] Therefore, we know success is possible.

- The Construction Industry Institute (CII) has identified seventeen best practices for the construction[44] industry (CII Best Practices, n.d.). These practices could significantly improve project performance, including cost, schedule, safety, quality, and operability.

On the other hand, we have seen the bad and the ugly.

In some cases, failed projects threatened the existence of the companies involved. Recently (2024), one of the leading contractors in Texas declared bankruptcy because of project troubles.

In this chapter, we will discuss:

1. Stats and references
2. Project success ambiguity
3. Diversity of practice
4. Fragmentation of project management
5. Other relevant topics

It is important to stress that each topic deserves a dedicated chapter (if not a short book). However, to maintain the focus, we will provide links to external resources if the reader wants more in-depth coverage.[45]

---

[43]   In the capital projects industry, a megaproject is commonly defined as a project costing more than one billion dollars (US).

[44]   In this context, the construction industry refers to capital projects and project management across the entire project life cycle, not just construction work.

[45]   These topics and others will be at the core of a follow-up book, Transforming Project Management.

Stats and References

Unfortunately, to our knowledge, no project management professional associations clearly define project or project management success (or failure). Without definitions, criteria, and scoring models, we end up with too many ambiguous reports and statistics that might not make sense. For example, some research on capital projects[46] shows that only 0.5% of the projects are successful, according to one study (Flyvbjerg & Gardner, 2023). Another shows that success could be as high as 60% (Barshop, 2016). Another reference classifies technology projects as successful, challenged, or failed. This reference[47] claims that about one-third of projects succeed while the others are challenged or fail.

> *Numerous surveys, studies, and references from organizations, universities, and institutes tell us that project failure is too common.*

When we were working on an earlier book, **Leading Megaprojects,**[48] we researched this topic extensively and reviewed many studies from different industries worldwide. These studies confirm the high rate of project management failures. However, the rate might vary from

---

[46] Capital Projects are also known as Capital-Intensive Projects and, in some references, Construction Projects. These projects often involve building an asset, facility, or factory that the project owner will own and run to generate value. They typically need significant capital investments, often millions or even billions.

[47] A few of my colleagues question this reference since they only share information in a proprietary state, and their method is not transparent. However, if we consider that they have been using the same method since the 1980s and show comparable results (with minor fluctuations), then we can consider the validity of their studies.

[48] Published in 2020 by CRC Press: https://urukpm.com/books/.

industry to industry, and the basis (baselines, reference points) used in their methods might vary.

Project Success Ambiguity

Project success is a hot and frequent topic on social media. The problem is that most posts talk about project success without any context. So, when some claim[49] 70% of projects fail, there are many problems with that. For example,

- We do not know if they are discussing a project failure (e.g., stopped projects or completed projects that did not deliver their goals) or a project management failure (e.g., cost and schedule problems).
- Commonly, these posts do not offer a source, or the source they provide is copying these claims from similar posts without basis. In other words, copy-paste without validation.
- Further, there is no mention of the method used or the reference points (i.e., is the comparison with an initial conceptual estimate or approved plan).
- There is no clarity on the definition of failure. For example, if the project's actual cost ended at 101%, is that a failure?

We know that this ambiguity does not cause projects to fail. However, it does not provide us with reputable and dependable studies that we can use to find the shared challenges and gaps. In response, UrukPM developed a model called the Four Dimensions of Project Success that recommends subdividing success into four dimensions to enable a

---

[49] This is a common claim that has been debunked many times.

focus on showing where the failure is happening. These are:[50] product technical success, project management success, product delivery success, and objectives success.

To help prove this point, we will ask you two questions (feel free to research):

1. Was the Sydney Opera House project a success or a failure?
2. How about the Euro Tunnel project? Was it a success or a failure?

When you answer these questions, consider the four dimensions. Would that help you find the problems?

Diversity of Practice

We were drafting a paper about Transforming Project Management.[51] As we were writing, it became critical to highlight a few vital points to ensure alignment and avoid misunderstanding. One of those points is the diversity of practice.

Unfortunately, various guides offer us generic project management definitions but with different interpretations depending on the context. Many of us often joke that the answers to most project

---

[50] We will only mention them briefly. For more information, start here: https://urukpm.com/the-four-dimensions-of-project-success/, and Chapter 13 in this book.

[51] We authored this paper for the UT Dallas Project Management Symposium 2023. Here is a copy: https://urukpm.com/wp-content/uploads/2020/09/transforming-project-management-while-respecting-our-diversity.pdf.

management questions must start with "It Depends,[52]" and there is a good reason for this.

For example, when we define a project and project management,

- Do we distinguish between projects for a service provider organization versus a project owner?
- Do we include the question of size and complexity in the project definition? For some, making a cup of coffee or going to dinner is a project; all we need is the right mindset. For others, projects could be business investments costing tens or hundreds of millions.
- Can we understand that managing a small and straightforward project requires a different approach than leading a large and complex one?
- Have we realized that most projects might share a set of processes, but a project management method should depend highly on the project type, size, and complexity?
- Speaking of methods, do we genuinely understand project management methods and their components?

The main point of the above is that there is diversity in the types of organizations using project management, and even within these organizations, there might be different approaches to leading projects. In a later chapter, we will discuss project management in industries. Here, we want to touch on a concept we call Project Management Levels.

---

[52] This link https://www.youtube.com/playlist?list=PLiXup1lJ-_TMd4xVfSot7lnvMpvn8X_ N5 is to a series of videos on the theme of "It Depends"

The PM Levels is about distinctive styles of leading "projects." Here is a list of these levels[53]:

1. Level 1 is the lowest (in terms of coverage and complexity) and is mostly about task management. Many low-cost and free tools can help this level.

2. Level 2 is broader than task management and involves managing a single project stage, typically following concepts like the PMI/ISO process groups[54]: initiating, planning, implementing, controlling, and closing. This approach is suitable for managing single-stage or small and simple projects.

3. Level 3 is technical project management and covers multiple stages. However, it often limits the project life cycle to starting with a project charter and ending with an output, ignoring what comes before the charter or after the output.

4. Level 4 concerns a product delivery model that would increase coverage and might include the work that would typically be pre-project charter. However, the project life cycle still ends with an output, the product.

5. Level 5 is the UrukPM value delivery methodology or equivalent model. In this model, we cover the entire project life cycle from ideation to initial operation, closing the project with a final success assessment.

---

[53] A recent webinar recording on this topic: https://youtu.be/rC4quAaswLA.

[54] Both the Project Management Institute® and the International Standards Organization (ISO) have guides that include the concept of process groups that must repeat in every stage. We will touch on this topic later in the chapter.

Project owner organizations, those that initiate the project and seek the benefits of its outcome, should work at level 5. That is the subject of Chapter 12.

Fragmentation of Project Management

This topic is central to our future book on Transforming Project Management. There are many examples of fragmentation, and we list and briefly discuss a few of them.

- **There are no links between project management and the business** (other organizational units). If there are some links, they might be weak and happen through poor interfaces. This might be due to the silos effect, lack of integration, absence of recognition of project management as an organizational function, etc.

  For example, Human Resources (HR) needs a new system (software). HR personnel might draft some requirements and pass them on to the Information Technology (IT) department. If IT has adopted project management, they might assign a project manager. Otherwise, they would only have a technical lead. IT can do the work internally or outsource to a vendor (one more party). When the IT department (or their vendor) finishes, they will hand over the product to HR.

  Frequent interaction between HR, IT, and other stakeholders is possible in some organizations. However, it is common to have silos, no single point of contact that follows the project from idea to operation, and it is likely to lack strong stakeholder engagement.

Many handover points along the project life cycle are possible. These could be from one unit to another and even to and from external providers and contractors. Handover and interfaces often include associated risks.

- **Lack of integration between project management and operations**: We have seen a widespread problem in limiting project management to the technical aspects of building a product (software, hardware, or facilities). Due to this limitation, the operational readiness aspects, including change management, are often absent or managed by a separate team, which might not be engaged until quite late in the life cycle.

  For example, the team building a hotel, a factory, or a software tool often differs from the team that must prepare for the operation, including hiring and training staff, marketing and communication, change management, etc. These teams are not only different; they often belong to internal and external entities or parties, each with hidden agendas and possibly conflicting interests.

- **PMO is often separated from project management (and too many types of PMOs)**. We will cover this in the next chapter.

- **Limiting project management thinking and roles to project manager**: In most industries, outside capital projects, we limit the project management work to the role of a project manager. In other words, no project management team or other team members support the project manager in leading the project. Please note that project management team members would be different from the technical team members doing the technical work (engineers, programmers, technical specialists).[55]

Other Relevant Topics

These topics reflect the current state of project management practice and contribute to the high rate of failures. Most are misunderstandings due to a lack of proper knowledge or education. Some are due to the commercialization and commoditization nature affecting project management. Further, some could result from a conscious conflict of interest, if not ethically questioned practices.

We will be brief!

Process Groups Versus Project Phases

One of the most popular guides on project management is the Guide to the Project Management Body of Knowledge® (PMBOK® Guide). This guide is one of the primary resources for the various certifications offered by PMI®, the Project Management Institute®. This guide, at least up to the sixth edition, included the concept of process groups. ISO 21500 offers a similar approach with minor changes in the names of the process groups.

A critical gap in practice is the confusion between the process groups and the project life cycle. The cause of the confusion is not an error in guides like the PMBOK® Guide or ISO 21500.[56] Many

---

[55] A relevant video: https://youtu.be/VeGUxQpgtUs

[56] We realize that the latest editions of these guides are evolving, and their current editions might differ from our writing.

practitioners and students of project management misunderstand these guides and apply what they believe they understand, resulting in less-than-optimal solutions.

An example of this situation is shown in the following illustration.

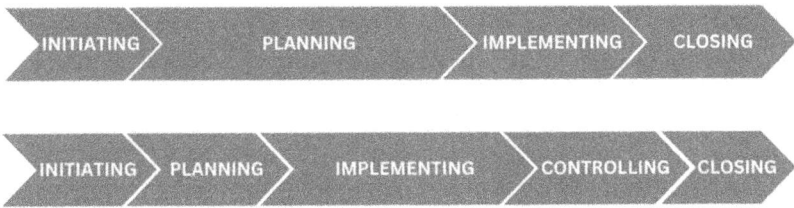

How some practitioners of project management understand the project life cycle (each row is a view)

Figure No 4.1: Some Practitioners View of the Project Life Cycle

These practitioners do not recognize two fundamental facts:

- The **process groups ARE NOT project phases**.
- These process groups repeat in every stage (phase).

Unfortunately, the situation is not limited to individuals; even some organizations label their projects' phases after the process groups and have adopted this as a project life cycle, labeling it the PMI® Methodology (although PMI® says it does not offer a methodology).

The issue is not the names and terminology. Whatever names individuals and organizations use for their project phases are not a problem as long as they understand that a *planning phase* differs from the *planning processes*. The *implementation phase* is not the same as *implementing processes*. Misunderstanding this vital distinction will have direct negative consequences on project performance.

Agile, agile, and agility

Another gap is the confusion between Agile, agile, and agility.

Agility is a necessity in organizations and on projects. However, agility is about being flexible, dynamic, and responsive to change. When we say an organization is agile, that would be agility. Therefore, agility is not about project management methods, although it is valuable for projects!

Agile is one of the most controversial topics today, with some Agile practitioners referring to themselves as Agilists or Agile Evangelists. The challenge is that these Agilists keep bending the definition to whatever suits them, even making false or unsubstantiated claims. In our view, Agile is not about project management methods. We restrict our view of Agile to the Agile Manifesto for Software Development, where Agile is about software development or product development, not management.[57]

Project Management Methods

One of the most critical gaps in practice is the confusion on project management methods—the too-frequent debate on waterfall versus agile directly results from this gap. Let us say our professional opinion here, knowing it is controversial:

- Waterfall is not a project management method; it is not logical.

---

[57] This video playlist is relevant to this topic: https://www.youtube.com/playlist?list=PLiXup1lJ-_TNMvGY7q3aix_cZBhMC_lUr

- As mentioned earlier, Agility and Agile are not project management methods.
- Hybrid is a made-up term that combines two concepts, which are not project management methods, yet we promote the integration of these concepts as a method.
- If you have time, we invite you to read the blog article referenced in the footnote.[58]

A related issue here is context, yes, context again. Here are a few examples:

What is a project management method?

- We use the terms method and methodology interchangeably, which is inaccurate.
- We use approaches or techniques on projects, and we call them project management methods—for example, critical path method, earned value method, and others. Therefore, the question is: what is a project management method?

Many practitioners think that what we just shared is a project management method—methods we use on projects—which is fine. However, remember that these are limited in scope to specific actions within a project.

Then, what is a project management method?

We touched on this topic earlier (Diversity of Practice) and will cover it extensively in Part B.

---

[58] https://blog.urukpm.com/?s=waterfall

Certifications

Many professional associations worldwide offer project management certifications, including introductory, advanced, generic, and specialized[59] ones. The number of certificate holders exceeds two or three million professionals. Some professionals have more than one certification from the same or multiple associations. Some of these certifications have existed for decades.[60] However, we have not found a credible, independent study proving that these certifications contributed to organizational success. On the contrary, as we shared earlier, the studies and surveys on project success do not show any notable improvement.

Why is that?

This is a significant question and requires a proper study, which is outside the scope of this book. What is relevant to this book is that the current state of practice with millions of certificate holders has not been effective, which is another reason to look for a substantial change.

To be clear and transparent, we are NOT saying that certifications do not offer value. It is likely that most, if not all, certifications from credible associations offer a great deal of value in learning. They might even help their holders with professional growth. So, the value to individuals can be taken as a fact. However, we are questioning their collective value to organizations and how that manifests in improved project success rates.

---

[59] For example, cost engineering, business analysis, scheduling, and risk management.

[60] The most popular certificate is the PMP® (Project Management Professional® offered by PMI®. In 2024, the PMP® would have existed for 40 years.

We recall a senior director in a government ministry telling me: *"Mounir, we have certified 50 individuals, and they still struggle in managing projects."* There are many reasons for this, such as:

- Passing a generic certification proves knowledge, not ability (competence).
- Most certifications do not offer or align with a methodology.
- Organizations that invest in certifications but do not change their processes or set up an organizational project management system would be like learning a new language you cannot practice, which is forgotten quickly!

Project Management versus Professional Project Management

My colleague, Trevor K. Nelson, posted an article on November 25, 2024. Trevor mentioned the following:

> *"I think the single biggest challenge we as 'project professionals' face is that we rarely make the distinction between project management and *professional* project management. And there *is* a difference."*

In support of the above statement, years ago, I was working on a mega project (the value of money in the 1990s was about $800 million). I worked hard to convince the project director to get a project management certification (I will not mention which) and finally convinced him. A few weeks later, he returned from a trip to the company headquarters. He was furious that an IT technician in their company with limited experience had achieved that same certification. So, he was raising the question about the value of this certification for a director on a mega project (or even a project manager for a large project, for that matter) if a junior technician (not a project manager) could achieve it.

Trevor indirectly addressed this point by saying:

> *"But as the project size, complexity, cost, importance, etc., increases, we move away from what an 'accidental' or 'halo effect' PM is capable of and into the realm where a 'professional' PM is required."*

Closing Remarks

We realize that executives might not be interested in the details of this chapter. However, we strongly recommend reading it. We did not include these topics to debate terminology or semantics. These topics are vital to understanding our challenges and problems. Accepting the problems allows us to shift our thinking to the solution. So, as an executive, you might not need to read all the papers/articles or watch the videos we referenced. However, we urge you to have your project management personnel or PMO directors review them and consider them as they develop the solution!

CHAPTER 5

Project Management Office

Introduction

In the earlier two chapters, we addressed:

- Inhibitors to project performance and
- The project management state of practice.

In this chapter, we continue with the state of practice. However, here, we focus on PMOs (project management offices). We see the idea of **PMO as a subset of the general project management function**. However, some practitioners often treat the PMO as a separate and independent domain from project management. We are not sure why, although we can guess that the driver behind this attempt to separate could be due to commercialization and consultancies selling services.

Earlier in the book, we mentioned that project management has an image problem, and we can say the same thing about PMOs (*see text box*).

It was common to find posts saying that PMOs are set to fail and that some have a short life. We realize this is not the case for all PMOs, and many of them have become indispensable for organizational success. However, we still see much confusion in the market about PMOs. There are debates questioning the PMOs' value and discussing their mandate, success, and maturity. In the Hidden Battle section of Chapter 1, we mentioned the pain of PMOs having to prove their value continually. We will discuss these topics in this chapter from different perspectives.

IMAGE PROBLEM

Professor Adam Boddison, the CEO of the UK's Association for Project Management, authored an article in 2023 for the association journal titled "Does project management have an image problem?" In that article, he said: "In truth, the project management profession has an image problem with leaders."

Here is a link to a LinkedIn post on the subject: https://www.linkedin.com/feed/update/urn:li:activity:7239282731833069569/.

These are the main topics:

1. PMO relevant information
2. The PMO Continuum
3. Why do some PMOs fail?
4. The executive factor
5. PMO pain points

PMO Relevant Information

Emergence of PMO

Project management's advancement and widespread acceptance led to the need for some formalization of the roles, which resulted in project management offices (PMOs). As a result, the 'PMO' acronym has become a recognized and quite popular term. Many organizations today have one form of a PMO or another. However, this term is still quite misunderstood, and these three letters could mean different things to different people. The reality is that not all PMOs are equal, which is Okay since, in this context, one size does not fit all. Let us explain.

First, what does the abbreviation PMO stand for?

There is no agreement in the industry on **one** standard definition of what these three letters mean. Most often, different organizations use the term to mean various things, including:

- Project Management Office: this is the most used term.
- Program Management Office: this is also a common definition.
- Portfolio Management Office: This is less common. An organization with a Portfolio Management Office might be called an ePMO ('e' for enterprise) or a cPMO ('c' for corporate).
- We have also heard the term PMO refer to 'PM Officer,' 'PM Organization,' or 'People Management Office', and other related terms.

Challenges and Confusions

Besides the name, there are other challenges and confusion. These include:

- **Is the PMO a temporary or permanent structure?**

  A temporary PMO would be like a PMO that an organization would set up to manage a single project or program. Practitioners in capital projects call these PMOs a project (or program) management team (PMT). So, this type of PMO exists today.

  This book discusses PMOs as **permanent organizational units that should be set up to "own" the project management function.** However, PMOs can take on different forms, roles, powers, and mandates.

- **Where should the PMO be positioned in the organization hierarchy?**

  Here, we might differentiate the PMO based on its role or mandate. For example, PMO at the corporate level is at a higher level, often reporting to a Chief Information Officer (CIO) or Chief Operation Officer (COO). In recent years, a few organizations have adopted the Chief Project Officer (CPO) position to lead the project management function.

  Alternatively, it is a widespread practice where the PMO sits within a department or division; often, it is the information technology (IT) department. However, a PMO could be anywhere in the organization's hierarchy.[61]

- **What is the type of PMO or its mandate/power?**

PMI® (The Project Management Institute)[62] suggests three types of PMOs: supportive, controlling, and directive. Some organizations refer to these types. However, we prefer an alternative concept; we believe in the PMO continuum, which we will discuss later.

Other associations and organizations offer different PMO types. Here are some examples: (1) linking the PMO to an organizational level, such as enterprise PMO, departmental PMO, or special purpose PMO. (2) others used the scope as a type of designator, such as skills-based PMO, project or program-based PMO, and process-based PMO.

- **Should the PMO include the delivery personnel?**

Some practitioners believe that project managers and project management team members who deliver projects should not be part of the PMO. In this case, a PMO should be limited to staff (analysts and specialists) who support the delivery but

---

[61] In one case, we were helping a client with PMO implementation. We discovered one of the challenges was about whom the PMO manager should report to, the COO or Deputy CEO. As we tried to understand and resolve the situation, the issue was not about the PMO role or mandate but about who the proposed PMO manager liked more (personal preference). That PMO failed within a year or two. Within ten years, that organization has set up and dismantled the PMO three times.

[62] In past editions of their Guide to the Project Management Body of Knowledge®

do not get directly involved. Other practitioners might have alternative views. There are a variety of models to consider.

- **Should the PMO be a service provider?**

We realize that many organizations, and many in the PMO community, believe that the PMO should be a service center/ service provider to the other organizational units. If we put on a customer-centric hat, this sounds like a great idea and aligns with the spirit of service, which is a good mindset if we are indeed a service provider. However, one of the triggers for authoring this book was to offer an alternative to this point.[63] We will leave the details for Part B.

Search for Identity

Due to past challenges and failures, which often continue to today's current state, the PMO community has been searching for a new identity. The search for identity might not be direct or conscious, but there are many indicators of this reality.

For example, instead of PMO, we have seen many organizations use terms like Vision Realization Office, Agile PMO, Digital PMO, Agile Management Office, Value Management Office, Value Delivery Office, and Transformation Management Office. Although these terms (offices) could imply some differences from a traditional PMO, once you drill down on the scope and mandate, you will find that they are (most of them) nothing more than different versions and names of a PMO.

[63]   A relevant video on the topic of customer-centric and service provider: https://youtu.be/1vw41ErQkMo.

We are willing to be skeptical here (although this might be a reality). The reason for the search for a new identity is a sign of failure of what existed, so some consultants/practitioners come up with a new label and a new idea to sell. In some cases, this is a form of deception and ethically questionable. For example, we recently posted a response to a post that mentioned something like this: *"Due to … PMO should now focus on generating value."* In this sentence, the "…" could be something like AI,[64] VUCA,[65] Complexity, Changing World, or you can fill in the blank.

What did we object to?

When the post mentioned that the community should now **shift** the focus to generating value, does that mean the earlier state (PMO, in this case) did not focus on value? If not, then why did it exist? What is the change?

We close this part by saying what should be obvious: Instead of rebranding and re-labeling, why don't we focus on finding and fixing the root causes?[66]

PMO Continuum[67]

As you will read in Part B of this book, **the proposed solution is to move beyond the idea of a PMO (and the different flavors of a**

---

[64]   AI = Artificial Intelligence

[65]   VUCA = Volatility, Uncertainty, Complexity, and Ambiguity

[66]   While updating this chapter, we found a post on LinkedIn where someone shared a 250+ pages guide titled: "From PMO to VMO." We must stress that we are not critiquing this guide; it could have great content. However, it supports our question that if we need to shift our thinking, what did the PMO (the previous state) offer?

[67]   This section is also relevant to the solution discussed in Part B.

PMO) into a higher, more practical (and effective) level, which is the vital need for organizations to recognize and accept project management as a core organizational function. This would be the final status of what organizations should aspire to. However, since we have not yet offered details about this proposed state, let us stay with PMO as the currently accepted norm.

We realize that there is no standard PMO. Further, depending on the organization's level of project management maturity, a PMO can start as a simplified entity and evolve over time. This is what we call the **PMO Continuum!**

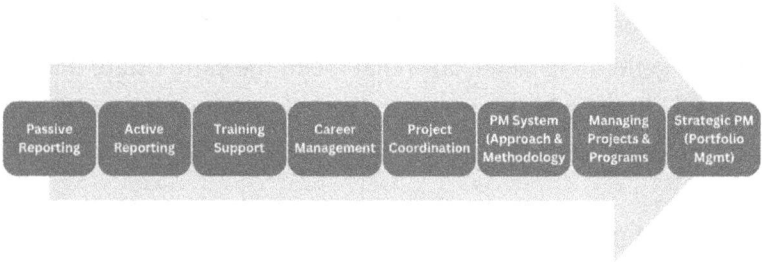

Figure No 5.1: The UrukPM PMO Continuum

The PMO Continuum represents the various functions and roles (focus/mandate) of the PMO within an organization. What we present below is likely in a logical order of importance. Still, since not all organizations are alike, the order we present is not likely the sequence all organizations follow. It is a broader model than limiting the view to supportive, controlling, and directive.

We will briefly explain each level below. However, please note that some PMOs, even those with broad mandates, might not include all these roles.

Passive Reporting

The most basic form and role of a PMO could be what we might call a 'Reporting PMO.' This PMO would collect reports from the various projects and programs, collate and summarize them, and then send a summary report to organizational management for review. In one case, we were invited to a leading regional bank (in West Asia) to support their people with their projects. When we were on site, someone mentioned they had a PMO, which we did not know. As we explored to learn more, it turned out that the PMO was an individual, the secretary of the department manager, whose job was to collect reports.

Active Reporting

One could present that since the PMO oversees reporting, it should also standardize the reports used by the projects and programs. Therefore, an active reporting PMO would set up standard guidelines for the project managers on the required reports. Notice that we are not mentioning where these reports go since that is a function of the PMO type and where the PMO is positioned in the organizational hierarchy.

Training Support

Suppose an organization starts to empower its PMO beyond its basic functions. In that case, the PMO can oversee reporting in addition to training and developing project management personnel (or at least send them to external generic training sessions). The idea here is not for the PMO to replace human resources or learning and development but for the PMO to work with learning and development to recommend the right professional training programs for the organization's project management staff.

Career Management

The next logical level could be for the PMO to assume responsibility for career management. Formal job descriptions and career paths for project management personnel across the organization should be set up in this case. This includes a professional development program that includes mentoring and coaching.

Project Coordination

In some organizations, the PMO might coordinate all or some of the organization's projects. The focus here is not on managing the projects but possibly coordinating between projects, managing the interfaces, and managing resource allocation.

Project Management System

This mandate might be limited to the PMO providing templates and not much more. However, in our professional opinion, one of the most crucial functions of a PMO is to assume responsibility for the organization's project management system. The PMO establishes the proper project management methods and processes. These would include things like:

- The processes to launch or initiate projects, plan for projects, and manage and control projects.
- A project management system should include a project management methodology.

- A captured lessons learned system.
- The PMO should also assume responsibility for the historical databases (may be included in reporting) and project records.
- It should also set up the performance metrics for projects.

Managing Projects and Programs

In some organizations, the PMO could also be the project management functional home for career project managers and project management personnel. When there is a project, the organization will pull the project manager from the PMO, and other project resources and team members will come from the other functional departments. This is a strong matrix organization for those with knowledge of project structures.

Strategic Project Management

This would be the highest level of a PMO, often considered a portfolio management office. In this case, the PMO might support the strategy formulation process or at least be involved in project selection.

Closing Comments

Our proposal is for organizations to adopt all the above (and much more) through a centralized, formally recognized function for effective and impactful strategy implementation. However, we offered the continuum as a practical alternative for gradually building the function. Similarly, a few organizations are offering some guidance on building PMOs. We are not endorsing or naming any of them; you will find them with a simple search if you want to stay with the current thinking of PMOs being service centers.

Why Do Some PMOs Fail?

PMOs fail for many of the same reasons that projects fail. There are many reasons (possibly symptoms). However, the root cause is the same: a lack of organizational recognition and acceptance of project management as a strategically important function that should be a core organizational function.

Here are some of the symptoms. It is a lengthy list, and we are not including many other factors:

- The copy-paste syndrome (copying forms and templates without alignment to the new context)
- Lack of clarity on PMO mandate
- Lack of understanding of PMO functions and roles
- PMO is sold by eager consultants (or internal staff) without understanding the organizational culture
- Lack of understanding of the strategic value of project management
- PMOs with limited authority or understaffed
- PMOs with poor leadership and lack of competent personnel
- *PMO leadership fails to help organizational leadership understand they don't "want X product," but instead they "want Y capability."*[68]
- *"PMOs that think they should and want to do "X," while leadership really needs them to do "Y." For example, a PMO that 'wants' to do portfolio management, but leadership 'needs' them to simply 'execute better.'"*[69]
- The absence of sponsorship, i.e., executive support

---

[68] This comment is from Joe Russell via a LinkedIn Post.

[69] This comment is from Trevor K. Nelson via a LinkedIn Post.

- Executives' lack of understanding of project management (the 4PMs[70]) and governance
- Lack of alignment between expectations and requirements
- Poor interfaces with the rest of the organizational units
- You can add to this list based on your experience.

In addition to the above, we asked our LinkedIn network for input on this topic. One colleague with decades of PMO experience, Mr. Trevor K. Nelson, shared the following:

"I think (for me) it comes down to two competing issues:

1. *A PMO community that thinks they don't need to improve and that it's really leadership's fault for not seeing the 'obvious' value and understanding how 'important' the PMO should be. (We rarely see a PMO say, 'Yeah, we need to get better').*
2. *A leadership view of 'anyone can manage projects, it's easy' (see 'accidental PM'),[71] so they don't understand why, if it's easy, the *professionals* aren't delivering better. So, we end up with PMOs wanting a bigger or more important role but not doing the 'original' things leadership wants, which would show their value and allow them to be considered for a larger role."*

---

[70]   Project, Program, Product, and Portfolio Management.
[71]   We discuss the accidental project manager syndrome in another chapter.

Here is another quotation from my good friend and colleague, Bill Duncan.[72]

> *"PMOs are created to "fix" project management. When they don't understand that, they fail."*

The following discussion builds on Duncan's point.

The Executive Factor

Here is our hypothesis about the scenario that triggers the request for a PMO Implementation.

Despite their many years of existence, we hypothesize that PMOs are still misunderstood, especially by executives who lack project management expertise or proper awareness.

Here is a scenario.

- Let us say company Z has had some issues, challenges, or even failures in implementing projects.
- Company Z executives have been hearing about project management and the value of project management.
- They also hear about this thing called "PMO."
- They hear about these things, maybe from a professional journal, an employee, or a consultant eager to sell services.
- With the above scenario, executives might decide to implement a PMO.

---

[72] Here is Bill Duncan's LinkedIn profile: https://www.linkedin.com/in/wrduncan3/. Duncan was the primary author of the PMBOK® Guide and has decades of expertise in project management standards, including with PMI®, IPMA®, and GPM®

Please pause and think about the following questions:

- What do the executives want?
- What triggers the request for a PMO?
- Why do they want a PMO?

In reality, executives want to improve the performance of their organizational projects. In their minds, executives want to deliver value to their shareholders, and the PM Office is only a mechanism.

What will the executive ask for?

Typically, the answer is a PMO Implementation because the client thinks (or is sold the idea) that the PMO will lead the performance transformation.

The fundamental issue here is that executives are asking for PMO … thinking … that they will have improved projects' performance. In other words, the requirements are for a PMO, but the expectations are improving performance. As you know, there are differences between expectations and requirements.

The executives' gaps and results

Executives do not realize that implementing a PMO (the office) with 1, 2, or more employees only structures an office for project management. This office might oversee reporting or a bit more (refer to the PMO Continuum). In other words, this office becomes another layer between management and project managers. In direct terms, this means more bureaucracy or policing force, which is a turn-off.

The Consequences

With the above, months later, or maybe a year or two later, the organization might accomplish improved reporting. However, project performance might not improve or only marginally improve (remember the wet towel from an earlier chapter). If the executives are patient enough and understand project management, they might assess the situation and see if a change in the PMO could solve the problems. If they are not patient enough, they will likely dismantle the PMO.

What could be worse?

Executives lose trust in project management.

The consequences are lost opportunity, wasted effort, and a damaged reputation, potentially leading to more projects failing or being challenged.

Remember the Hidden Battles from Chapter 1!

PMO Pain Points

In closing this chapter, we will raise a few points that could be from the PMO perspective.

- What obstacles do PMOs have in aligning projects with the company strategy?
- How can they manage resources across multiple projects?
- What is possible to minimize the resistance to change?

- How can the PMOs improve communication with the stakeholders?
- Is it possible to spend less time on administrative tasks and more time doing things that add value?
- The emerging challenge of AI and the associated risks of losing their job due to AI hype or reality?
- How can the PMOs gain sponsorship and executive support?
- How does the PMO demonstrate value? Did it provide improved project outcomes as well as an increasing success rate?
- What must we do to get a seat at the table (take part in decisions about future projects)?
- Why must we continue to prove our value (i.e., why executives do not trust us)?

Please re-read this list with the following mindset: can the PMO achieve these things without the proper mandate, executive support, and authority?

Closing Comments

In this chapter, we addressed the current state of practice, focusing on PMOs. We shared information about PMO emergence, challenges, and confusion. We also shared a view of the PMO continuum and reasons for PMO failure. Further, we shared a scenario about the executive factor and the gaps between expectations and requirements. Finally, we closed with a few pain points from the perspective of the PMOs (directors and personnel).

If your organization wants to implement a PMO, please read this chapter carefully to avoid some of the challenges related to

PMO implementation. Setting up a PMO is a real project, and it requires a deep knowledge of change management and financial analysis for possible future value and benefits evaluation. Being a project, it must be managed in accordance with a project management methodology.

However, we ask you to be patient since, in Part B, we will help you envision a future that goes beyond the PMO.

CHAPTER 6

Project Management in Industries

Introduction

We often say that many project management processes are generic or industry-agnostic—there are many similarities. However, there are often significant differences in practice, especially when considering the product type the project will deliver. For example, a generic concept tells us that we need to have cost estimates on projects. However, it does not tell us if we need one or more estimates and when along the project life cycle we need to develop these estimates; a project management method will give us that information.[73]

Therefore, it is essential to understand these differences and learn about concepts like the project management levels necessary to respect our diversity (shared in an earlier chapter) and the required methodological process that must be tailored, customized, and adapted—more on this in Part B.

This chapter will highlight some critical differences in project management practice. However, we must emphasize that sharing

---

[73] For example, it is common to have only one estimate on technology-centric projects. On capital projects, the project owner organizations would likely have three estimates along the project life cycle, and that would be before reaching the implementation stage.

these differences aims to understand them and identify cross-learning and knowledge transfer opportunities.

Industries

Some practitioners prefer terms like sectors, verticals, or domains as alternatives to industries, so we will use industries to avoid switching terms.

Numerous industries use project management today, including pharmaceuticals, medical, manufacturing, energy, academia, chemicals, utilities, and financials. Project management is also practiced in government, semi-government, non-governmental organizations, charities, and not-for-profit organizations. Each of these organizations offers a different context and has unique environmental factors affecting the practice of leading change initiatives, i.e., projects and programs.

We must emphasize and repeat a crucial point. All these organizations benefit from generic, shared project management practices. However, each has a uniqueness that is crucial for project success.

Types of Projects

Numerous variables could affect how one defines a type of project. For example, size, complexity, and industry. However, if we shift our thinking from industries, we can see the following practical types (also see the text box on How we label projects):

HOW WE LABEL PROJECTS?

One non-conventional idea is that organizations have one type of project, which is a business project. The intent here is that most (if not all) projects have business triggers. However, we often talk about IT projects and construction projects. In other words, we categorize projects based on their dominant type of work (technology, construction, marketing). The same thing in government and development sectors.

- **Capital Projects**[74]: These would be projects that require significant investment. In addition to a business case, feasibility study, and requirements stages, these projects will often require engineering and construction and lead to a physical facility (house, clinic, hotel, power plant). These projects exist in various industries.

- **Technology Projects**: There are many subcategories in technology, including hardware and software. Like capital projects, these technology projects, especially software, exist in most industries.

- **General Projects**: These could be projects from any industry, but they are mostly related to business or operations, such as process improvement, marketing, and training.

---

[74] Also known as construction projects.

- **Other types**: There are other specialized types from different industries, such as logistics, supply chain, medical research, and defense. However, most of them will fit into the three categories we listed. Those that do not fit would be outside the scope of this discussion (specialized cases).

For the rest of this chapter, **it is more practical to address variables related to these types instead of industries.**

Diversity of Practice

Are there differences in how organizations (in the various industries) oversee their projects?

Can we learn from each other and transfer knowledge across fields of practice?

Yes, and we will list a few examples to raise awareness.

PMOs

Organizations predominantly working on capital projects might not have PMOs unless they use the term instead of a project management team (refer to temporary PMOs in the earlier chapter). Instead of PMOs, these organizations would have project management departments or divisions.[75] Some large organizations could have an entire business unit with multiple departments dedicated to project management. In one company we worked with, the project

---

[75] We share a couple of case studies in a later chapter.

management business unit (headed by a vice president) had close to 3,000 employees and contractors split among 8 or 9 departments.[76]

On the other hand, organizations focusing on technology or general projects often have PMOs or no formal project management unit at all. It is important to note that PMOs (as a concept) started within IT (Information Technology) departments, which helps explain the above. PMOs are still a recent concept, though some formality has existed for capital projects since the early 1900s.

Over the years, we have seen higher levels of maturity and better performance in organizations that formally recognize project management. One of the primary triggers behind this book is to extend the benefit of a formally recognized project management function.

Core or Supporting Function

Let us ask:

Is project management a core and formal organizational function or primarily a support function? (*See text box about "formal"*).

Organizations with (large) capital projects often consider project management a formal function, equal to the other organizational functions, and represented through a formal business unit (like HR, IT, or Finance)[77]. The personnel in these departments would be career project managers and specialists (planners, cost engineers, schedulers, and construction staff).

---

[76]   This number excludes the engineering and construction contractors' personnel working on projects where it is common to have 5000+ construction workers on a single project.

[77]   Where this exists, it is close to what we are proposing in Part B.

WHAT DO WE MEAN BY "FORMAL"?

We are using the term "formal" in this context to refer to an organizational unit that is formally recognized, typically by a board of directors. It would be set up as a department or division well-defined within the organizational hierarchy and system and follow certain rules of governance.

On the other hand, a semi-formal or even informal unit would be something like an executive would set up and the same executive (or another) can dismantle, without board approval. Although this type of structure might have some governance, it would not be at the level of the formal unit.

On the other hand, in other organizations working on technology or general projects, project management might not exist as a separate unit or have one form of PMO or another. If they have a PMO, it would be rare for it to be formal, per our definition, although it might appear that way. In these situations, accidental project manager syndrome is widespread (more on this in the next chapter). Further, for those who become human resources or marketing project managers, it is likely a transition (or temporary) role before they move on to something else.

Project Life Cycle Management

Some organizations working on capital projects often follow formal, well-defined methodological processes, like a stage gate model. Some might even utilize best practices like those of the Construction Industry Institute (CII, https://www.construction-institute.org/). In these situations, a few project owner's organizations would have built the capacity and competence to lead their projects. In contrast, those not invested in project management might use Project Management Contractors/Consultants (PMCs) to lead the projects on their behalf. In either case, the project life cycle often covers projects from business case to initial operations, with an executive responsible for the entire life cycle to minimize the effect of silos. If we relate this to the project management levels discussed in an earlier chapter, these could be levels 3, 4, or 5.

If we shift our thinking to general or technology projects, project management is often highly fragmented with no well-defined project life cycle. In most cases, these organizations might not know anything about a stage gate model. Further, they often miss the idea of a single point of accountability, even when they have a project sponsor. Project management levels 1 and 2 are the dominant practice in these situations.

Single Point of Accountability

In line with the previous point, capital projects' organizations often have a project executive as the single point of accountability for the project from ideation to operation. This would help maintain the consistency and focus across the project life cycle and minimize the effect of silos.

On the other hand, this is not as common as it should be in technology and general projects, even when the organization uses the concept of project sponsors.

Silos

All organizations have different divisions/units involved in each project. The question is, then would these become silos with minimal interfaces and collaborations? This is often highly dependent on organizational culture. However, within capital projects, there is often some collaboration along the life cycle; the degree of collaboration varies from loose to solid integration. Meanwhile, in other projects, the project might not even be considered a project until it reaches the IT department (or a vendor).

Project Management Team

Years ago, we led project management training courses. When the audience was primarily those working on general or technology projects, and we mentioned the idea of a project management team, the attendees were often confused. They had heard the term project team but never the project management team. To them, there was only one role: the project manager. The rest were team members working on product development (software, programming, web, etc.). In this context, the project manager was responsible for everything, such as estimating, planning, risk and change management, communication, design, and even influencing upward.

On the other hand, on capital projects, it is rare to see project management limited to the role of the project manager, even on small projects. There is much complexity and diversity of the needed expertise. As a result, in this context, we have project management teams, even on small projects (see text box regarding PM vs. PMT). We had project engineers, construction engineers, safety, quality, cost, planning, project control, and other roles whose primary focus was project management within their specialty.

PROJECT MANAGER VS. PROJECT MANAGEMENT TEAM

Earlier in my career, I was assigned as a project engineer* at a chemical plant to manage multiple small projects**. In that role, I often worked on 5-10 projects at any given time. Some were in front-end planning***; others were in the engineering, construction, or commissioning stage. So, I was a full-time project manager working all the projects but working part-time on each of those projects. However, I was not alone. We had cost estimators, quality inspectors, safety personnel, project control specialists, and construction engineers.

The point here is that project management involves numerous skills, and often, a project manager does not have all the necessary skills. The capital project industry understands this challenge and supports the project manager with a project management team. However, outside capital projects, we think the project manager must be the expert capable of doing it all, like the jack-of-all-trades but the master in none.

* In that context, a project engineer is a project manager.

** These projects' costs ranged from about $200,000 to $2 million.

*** Front-end planning refers to the stages from ideation to final funding (before detailed engineering).

So, can technology and general projects benefit from similar arrangements, as appropriate?

Product Development

In capital projects, the product development work (i.e., designing and building the product), with the final product being a facility, we often need some sequential development approach (with some overlap) that would lead to delivering the output (i.e., the product) in one significant handover, Big Bang style.[78]

The other types (general and technology) can often use agile development concepts like iterative and incremental development.

Closing Remarks

Regardless of your industry or the type of projects you oversee, it is vital to understand and respect our differences. We must embrace value as the core goal of our methodological processes. We need to shift from thinking about project management as a supporting role to allowing the integration of project management with the rest of the organizational functions!

We leave you with some questions:

- Can we cross-learn from each other?
- Can we find great practices in one domain and see if we can apply them in another while respecting diversity and unique factors?
- Does one industry (or type of project) do better than the others?

---

[78] Some in the project management community call these predictive methods.

CHAPTER 7

Project Management and the C-Suite

Introduction

Over the last few decades, project management has seen significant growth and acceptance across sectors, industries, and domains. Project management skills are in demand across organizational levels. Various professional associations and private companies offer numerous certifications in project management—more than one hundred. It would be safe to say that more than a few million practitioners have one project management certificate or another.

Furthermore, in 2016, we witnessed the government of the United Kingdom recognizing project management by granting chartered status to the Association of Project Management. The same year, the UK government also formed the Infrastructure and Projects Authority (IPA). The United States also passed a law for project and program accountability within the US government. The European Commission uses a project management methodology. Further, PM4NGOs is an organization that focuses on NGOs and the development sector and offers a methodology.

Nevertheless, projects continue to fail or face many challenges.

Individuals and organizations do not realize that this current practice is not sustainable. They do not fully understand that the causes include a lack of standardized processes, missing methods or methodological approaches, no project management system, and, quite often, no executive support or sponsorship.

Organizations launch projects, and it is common to hear project managers complain about a lack of sponsorship. Is this the responsibility of the project managers or the sponsors and executives?

Challenges, The Executive Reality

Many executives still have not recognized, accepted, or respected project management enough to make it a formal and permanent function in their organizations. For example, positions such as chief project officer or head of projects are still exceedingly rare. Also, project management departments outside the capital projects industries are rare. There are project management offices (PMOs)[79]. However, as discussed earlier, some PMOs fail or fall short of fundamental transformation.

It is still expected to observe accidental project manager's syndrome with the mindset that anyone can manage projects. Still, when it comes to finance, strategy, engineering, human resources, or marketing, these organizations insist on hiring or training specialists

---

[79] We have seen different reports discussing the percentage of organizations with PMOs, and the numbers vary. The PM Solutions 2020 study has the number at 79% on average. A Statista 2020 report states that 82% of organizations worldwide have one or more PMOs.

with a background in these domains. It would be rare for an organization to ask an engineer to do the accounting or an accountant to carry out a marketing campaign.

Furthermore, we observe organizations that might invest in training their staff on project management topics. Management even encourages or mandates their employees to achieve one certification or another. However, they do not invest in building proper, comprehensive, sustainable, and effective project management systems for their organization's various functions. Some organizations think a two-, three-, or five-day class would be enough to "master project management."

Unfortunately, some professional associations have pushed their certifications to become a commodity, where young and inexperienced professionals can follow a packed study program and become certified without having managed a project in their career or personal lives. It is also common for some individuals to memorize a standard or study guide without knowing how to apply the concepts to an actual, even simple project.

In the earlier chapters, we provided details about inhibitors to performance, the current state of project management, and project management offices. We also discussed the diversity of practice in the last chapter. We want to move beyond the Hidden Battles addressed in Chapter 1. Therefore, in this chapter, we are shifting the focus to the role of executives and directors (management).

Pain Points From a Management Perspective

In the PMO chapters, we mentioned some pain points from the perspective of PMO directors and staff. Here, we are offering some pain points from the perspective of executives.

- Confusion due to the chaos in the market and the hype that often occurs leads to uncertainty about what to do: offer training and certifications, build a PMO, outsource, or something else.
- How can we improve performance and align projects to strategy?
- Why is project management an office, not a department? In other words, should project management be recognized as a formal function? Also, do organizations need a chief project officer?
- When should project management be involved in projects? Should project management be involved at the strategic level, even in strategy formulation?
- View project management as a transaction/operation rather than a strategic skill set. Alternatively, should they consider projects as business investments?

We are sure there are many issues, questions, and pain points. The bottom line and the most crucial factors are the results. Many in management might not care about project management (the mechanism); their concern is results. If we want to go from point A to point B, it might not matter how; we could walk, ride a bicycle, take a bus, or drive. If all that matters is getting to point B, then sure, the mechanism might not matter. However, in business and on projects, the mechanism often matters.

Therefore, we advise that management take a step back and evaluate the current state. Assess the options to identify the most effective mechanism. Organizations need project management to implement strategies effectively and maximize shareholder value!

Strategy Implementation

Question 1

We often hear organizations have no problem formulating strategies but fail in implementation. Is there any research on this?

Substantial research indicates that many organizations struggle more with strategy implementation than formulation. Here are some key insights:

- **Harvard Business Review**: A study published in HBR highlights that while many organizations excel at developing strategies, they often falter in execution. The study emphasizes the importance of aligning organizational structure, culture, and resources with the strategic plan (Favaro, 2015).

- **PwC's Global PPM Survey** reveals that only 2.5% of companies successfully complete 100% of their projects. The primary reasons for failure include poor communication, lack of leadership, and inadequate resource allocation (Saalmuller, 2022). Many of the reasons are directly or indirectly related to effective project management.

- **Others**: Here, we include titles of other reports: (a) The gap between formulation and implementation often arises from a lack of coordination and adaptability; (b) The success of implementation hinges on the ability to synchronize all departments and teams.

These studies underscore the importance of having a well-thought-out strategy and ensuring the organization can execute it effectively.

Question 2

Can project management help with strategy implementation?

Project management is crucial in bridging the gap between strategy formulation and implementation. Here are some ways it can help (we are only sharing the list):

- Alignment of projects with the strategic goals
- Structured planning and execution
- Resource management
- Risk management
- Performance management
- Stakeholder engagement
- Change management
- Governance and accountability

By integrating these project management practices, organizations can enhance their ability to execute strategies effectively and achieve their strategic objectives.

The Role of Executives

Let us emphasize a paragraph from the Hidden Battles of Chapter 1.

"Shifting our attention to executives, we notice the following: A few executives might see project management as a transactional or operational domain, and what exists is okay, i.e., there is no need for change. Some executives discuss the need for project management but do not see how to achieve success; there is too much noise and confusion in the community. Some believe project management is critical but lacks a clear, impactful path. Others see delays, problems, budget overruns, quality issues, and nightmares, so they question the value. Consequently, some executives lose trust in project management and their PMOs to the point where some go as far as questioning the need for projects or project management. Consequently, they are waiting for their PMOs to prove their value."

We can relate to the executive's frustrations, confusion, or position if we read the above positively. After all, we (in the project management community) failed. Therefore, we must understand the executives' view and accept our shortcomings.

> *If we continue with the above blame game, we might be caught in a cycle of doom.*

On the other hand, if we read it with a critical mindset, we can conclude that this might be a situation where the blame shifts to

PMOs and the project management staff. It is like executives are absolving themselves from responsibility or accountability.

It is vital to know the following: without an understanding and appreciation among leadership teams for the strategic value competent project management brings, it will never gain appropriate priority and resourcing. We need executives to trust and empower project management while continuing to hold the project management resources accountable. Further, executives must understand that they need to support, guide, sponsor, and provide a level of authority to project managers and PMOs.

The Risk of the Accidental Project Manager

We share an article we wrote years ago. It is also one of our e-books. This article highlights a scenario that is directly relevant to the point of this chapter, which is the role and responsibility of executives.

The Definitions

An accidental project manager is a term for a professional who "stumbled upon" project management when their managers ask them to manage a project, often without background, education, training, or experience in project management.

Many project managers today started as accidental project managers. Therefore, there is nothing wrong with the concept; it is how we manage it.

The Challenge to Executives

In one of our earlier books, *Redefining the Basics of Project Management*, we raised a "point to ponder" or a challenge to executives. We wanted to trigger executives to consider the risks associated with the concept of the accidental project manager and reconsider the situations that lead to appointing accidental project managers. We do not want to eliminate the conditions; we want executives to ponder how to minimize the threats effectively and maximize the opportunities caused by this syndrome.

Once again, we must stress that we are not against the concept. We have a problem with how it is used.

Project management is a dynamic field; some label it "an emerging profession" where many practitioners do not have formal education or training in project management.[80] Many of its practitioners are technical or functional specialists who are dependable professionals. As a result, these professionals are trusted to manage projects for one reason or another. Further, executives expect them to perform in the new role as project managers at the same level they have performed in their field of study. This is what we call "the accidental project manager syndrome."

Considering the above, the point to ponder–the challenge–is:

Do you agree that the above practice is common?

---

[80] It is still uncommon to find project management university programs, especially at the bachelor level. Further, many degree programs, including engineering and business, do not offer courses in project management or offer them as electives.

Let us expand on the previous question:

1. Why do you think executives and senior managers assign non-project managers and those without training or education in project management the responsibility to manage projects?
2. Why do you think these executives expect the accidental project managers to perform in project management at the same level as their performance in their educational or professional domain?

As an executive, do you have answers to these questions?

More to Consider

Let us look at these questions from different angles.

- Would we visit a hospital administrator for a medical checkup or surgery?
- Would you go to a legal assistant to defend you in court?
- Would you even go to a butcher shop to buy your bread?
- Do you ask a marketing major to fix a computer?

If we do not do any of these things, why do we assign project management to people other than project managers and continue to expect good or even excellent performance?

More questions:

- Can an excellent practicing civil engineer immediately step up and manage the development of a significant structure or facility?
- Can a sound computer engineer manage a major telecommunication infrastructure project?
- Can a human resource expert suddenly manage an organizational change project?

We agree that many technical and functional professionals can learn how to manage projects—and some become experts and produce amazing results. However, they must be professionally trained before the assignment and not learn under fire or be put into a sink-or-swim situation; the possibility and price of failure are incredibly high for the individual and the organization.

We make these decisions and then wonder why projects fail—or, to be more politically correct, we should say "why projects are not successful!"

Closure

What do you think?

- Do you think the concept is acceptable under any condition? ... or ...
- The concept is not acceptable under any condition. ... or ...
- The concept is acceptable given certain conditions. In this case, what do you think the conditions should be?

Now, let us add a bit of complication and think of these two scenarios:

- An organization has no formal project management, PMO, OPM (organizational project management) system, or methodology. What would be the consequences of the accidental project manager?
- An organization has formal project management, PMO, OPM system, and a well-defined methodology. What would be the consequences of the accidental project manager?

Which of these scenarios is the riskier one?

Closing Remarks

The image below is a modified version of an initial sketch by a friend and colleague, Mr. Nah Wee Yang[81] of Knowledge Method, Singapore. Wee Yang sketched as we delivered a workshop on organizational project management.

Although the sketch focuses on organizational culture, we find it relevant to our topic in this chapter since it mentions organizational processes as three-dimensional. Although each of the three dimensions might have different direct owners, they all lead back to the executives and organizational management.

Management must recognize the gaps in these three process areas and lead the transformation when needed. Yes, results count. However, we cannot succeed without people, processes, and technologies.

Organizational Culture can lift us or hold us down!

---

[81] Here is Wee Yang's LinkedIn profile: https://www.linkedin.com/in/weeyang/.

Is your organizational culture
pulling you DOWN or lifting you UP?

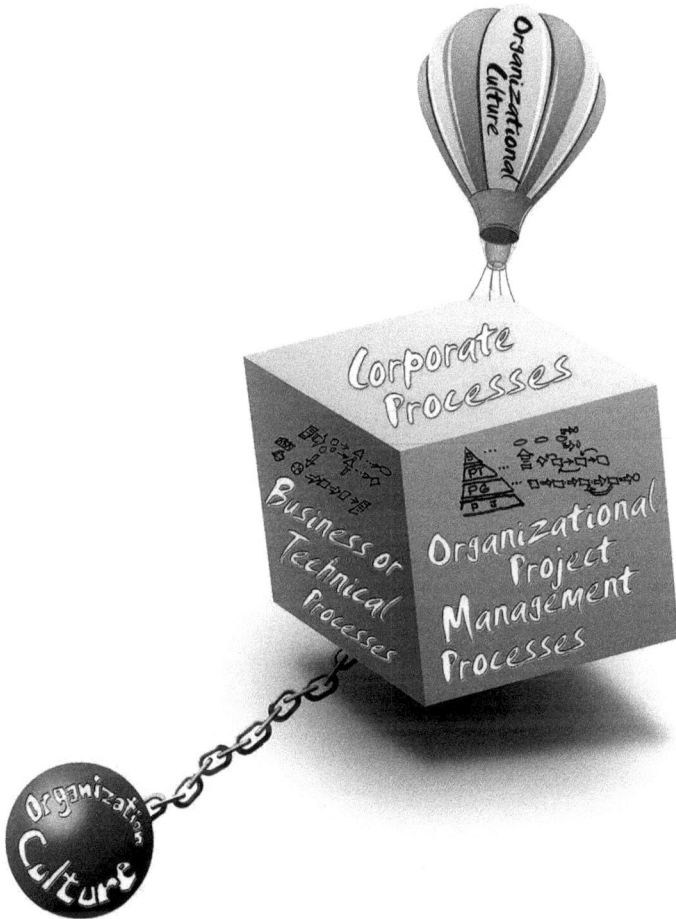

PART B

The Envisioned Future

Introduction to Part B

This part of the book covers the envisioned future and our proposed change.

Like Part A, we subdivided this topic into chapters to address the various critical elements of the solution. These include:

- Chapter 8, **The Case for Change**: By presenting the current state in Part A, we indirectly made a case for change. However, we still need this chapter. We need it to emphasize the importance of shifting our paradigm. We need organizations to shift their thinking from project management as a transactional, supporting role to recognizing it as an essential organizational function. Ensuring project success requires significant effort in terms of people, processes, and technology. Predetermined success results from the effort of project teams and the executives' vital support and sponsorship.

- Chapter 9, **Project Management as a Function**: In Part A, we introduced the solution in two vital parts; the first part is the project management function, which is the subject of this chapter. Here, we stress shifting our thinking from PMOs and their various flavors and concepts to a centralized, recognized, influential, and practical project management function. This is necessary to transform project management and enable impactful strategy implementation. Over decades of global experience, we have experienced and learned that organizations with a higher level of project management maturity excel and achieve excellent results. Therefore, this chapter will discuss our views on the project management function and associated divisions, including structure and mandate.

- Chapter 10, **Visualize the Future**: This chapter supplements the previous chapter and is vital to understanding the envisioned future. It provides a visual of the partnership at the executive level between the various executives and project management led by a chief officer. We also provide additional details to help executives understand this topic and how they can significantly enable the transformation. It is like a "day-in-a-life" of the future of work.

- Chapter 11, **Integrations to Deliver Value**: The second part of the solution is countering the existing fragmentation and working toward integrations as a necessity for Vision Realized! It is a fact that a persistent problem in today's practice is separating project management from the rest of the business. A related problem often involves treating each project independently, separated from its context or organizational impact. Here, we address the need for horizontal and vertical integrations as an essential context for the effective delivery of products, completion of projects and programs, and managing the entire portfolio.

- Chapter 12, **Value Delivery**: We have stressed the need for impactful strategy implementation enabled by project management and the need for projects and programs as the mechanism for successful change. Therefore, it is essential that we consider our value delivery methodology the engine of success. The focus is on integrating the project life cycle with the rest of the organizational function, from ideation to operation. This methodological process is the subject of decades of effort, collaborating with clients and delivering workshops and other content. Detailed coverage of this methodology, which we summarize here, can be found in our 2017 book, **Project Management Beyond Waterfall and Agile**.

- Chapter 13, **Project Success**: This chapter presents the Uruk Four Dimensions of Project Success, which our team developed in 2010. This is one of the core topics of transforming project management (the subject of our next book). However, we know it would be valuable to include as the last chapter in this part to help executives visualize a critical concept for project and portfolio success. We developed this model to cover a gap in practice in 2010. Unfortunately, that gap continues today!

CHAPTER 8

The Case for Change

Introduction

Can project management be a competitive advantage?

We say yes and add that **project management is indispensable for organizational success!**

We recall a conversation with a senior director from a government ministry (about 20 years ago): "*Mounir, we certified about 50 people, and they still struggle to manage projects.*" Another executive said, "*We have implemented a PMO but shut it down because we did not see any improvement. The only difference was that failure became more visible.*"

The above statements reflect the challenges and pains we continue to experience in organizations. They highlight the failed investments, (a) in certifications, (b) PMO implementations, and (c) the continual failure and challenges of projects. These situations lead to hidden battles. They create uncertainty, confusion, chaos, and sometimes, lost trust in a strategically important domain like project management.

In earlier chapters, we admitted our failures to deliver results in the project management community, contributing to the lost trust. We are letting incompetence and poor practices overshadow our mindset. This is generalizing, like saying, "Teenagers are trouble just because a few might be delinquent."

We ask you to consider the following: imagine a company losing money. Do they fire the finance department?

It is time to reverse the current reality and focus on the half-full part of the glass.

Enough with the self-scolding.

What we need is a change in thinking.[82]

We need to show our readers that project management can be a competitive advantage and that we can predetermine success! We must highlight our successes and share how many organizations have succeeded in leading their projects and portfolios.

When we shared that only 2.5% of companies deliver all projects successfully (PwC, 2014), we focused on the low score as a horrible indicator. However, can we see the value that those 2.5% of companies achieve when they realize success on all change initiatives? When we think of the 35% success rate of megaprojects, we zoom in on the low percentage, and we see 65% failed projects and billions of dollars in losses. Yet, 35% succeeded in delivering value! In megaprojects,

---

[82] A relevant video on the case for change: https://youtu.be/C8QeF7E7mxU.

some successful projects leave a legacy and significant economic opportunity for decades.

Therefore, success is possible.

We can predetermine, cultivate, and achieve success.

We can realize benefits and deliver shareholders value.

How?

Through individual competence.

With a higher level of project management maturity.

… and … most importantly, through system thinking.

… and … it must be a partnership.

That is why we advocate for change, a transformation!

We must have faith supported by reality, dedication, and the mindset of Vision Realized!

Insanity

Traditionally, some organizations train people and send them to acquire generic certifications. Then, they wonder why the training or certifications did not leave notable organizational value (see Two Stories text box).

Other organizations implement PMOs that might not have enough authority or the proper mandate. When a PMO fails, some look for a "rebrand" rather than identifying the root causes. They blame methodology, people, or the weather when a project fails.

An analogy would be when we treat significant injuries with band-aids and manage the associated pain with off-the-shelf medications. We have been doing this for years and decades, yet we are not seeing any significant improvements.

TWO STORIES

Once, a client asked us to deliver an "X" Certification training for construction. We told him this "X" certification is generic and does not directly address construction. We lost the contract.

In another situation, a client in the same domain (construction) came to us after many failed training sessions and asked us to deliver "X" certification training. However, this executive recognized the generic nature of this certification. Therefore, he asked us to include (add) practical, practical training specific to construction work.
Which company do you think achieves better results?

"Insanity is doing the same thing over and over again and expecting different results." This definition[83] encapsulates the idea that repeating

---

[83] The definition of insanity is often attributed to Albert Einstein. However, it's important to note that this quote's attribution to Einstein is debated, and there's no concrete evidence

the same actions without variation is unlikely to yield different outcomes and highlights the importance of innovation and change.

Once again, it is time for a change in thinking to seek a sustainable transformation.

Imagine

As an executive, do you think there is room for improvement even in organizations doing well on projects?

What can you do if you are in an organization with frequent challenges and even project management failures? Can you sustain these challenges? Can you continue to tolerate these pain points?

What do you need to sleep better at night and enjoy your dreams while avoiding nightmares?

If you could transform the current state, would you not enjoy winning often?

How about your staff and teams? Would they be proud of being part of an organization that consistently produces success? Wouldn't this be motivational and reduce stress and turnover?

With increased competence, organizations can achieve more success; success is motivational; motivations drive more success, and success benefits all (teams, executives, and shareholders). In

---

that he said it. However, the point is still valid regardless of who said it first.

other words, would it not be great to grow and prosper instead of being trapped in a cycle of doom?

A Point to Ponder

This point might seem sidetracking, but ponder it and hold on to that thought.

Can you kill your organization's human resources (HR), information technology (IT), finance, or engineering departments?

If you cannot kill them, can you downgrade them to …

Another side of this question is this:

Why are HR, IT, and other functions often organized as departments (formal[84] organizational functions) but project management is only an office[85] (assuming you have a PMO)?

Think about the following:

- What differences would be between an HR division and an HR office?
- Would fundamental differences exist if we had a finance division versus a finance office?
- If you are in an organization where engineering is essential, can you downgrade engineering to an office from a division?

---

[84] Formal refers to the board of directors' recognition and inclusion in organizational systems, hierarchy, and governance.

[85] Some practitioners (and readers) would say, "Well, the PMO is a formal department." Is it? Check again: Who set up the PMO, and who can dismantle it?

This point is not about semantics or names. It is about governance, recognition, acceptance, and understanding the value of these various functions.[86]

Demonstrating Success

If we change, would we have a better tomorrow?

Yes, we are confident.

We will say, "Trust us," and provide the supporting facts, as shown below.

We emphasize that we are building on the idea of:

Project management is a competitive advantage; it is indispensable for organizational success.

Here is what we know: **competent project management in mature organizations** can deliver the following[87]:

- A significant increase in speed to market, up to 30%, and projects will be 2.5x more likely to be on budget and on time (Stage Gate International, 2024).
- Independent Project Analysis benchmarking data show that following the proper methodological process[88] could lead to

---

[86]   It is important to understand the context: these points concern organizations large enough to have these divisions or departments.

[87]   The keywords in this phrase are "competent" and "mature."

[88]   Such as a project life cycle/stage gate model.

a 5% increase in the expected net Present Value (NPV) versus a reduction of up to 45% if no method is followed.[89]

- One organization (confidential) targets 90% success; they want 90% of their projects to be completed with the cost and schedule targets (parameters ~ +/- 10%), and they regularly achieve this goal.

- In Chapter 2, we also shared the results of the University of California Berkeley study that links success to organizational project management maturity.

- The following image (Figure No 8.1: Project Management Maturity and Performance) is from PM Solutions, which shows similar correlations between organizational project management maturity and performance.

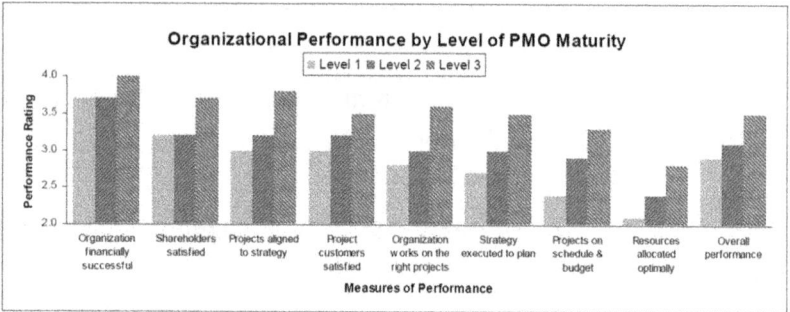

Figure No 8.1: Project Management Maturity and Performance

The Proposed Solution

This book proposes a solution as the starting point to achieve impactful strategy implementation and transform the project management state of practice.

---

[89] We shared an example in an earlier chapter where we quantified the benefits based on this study.

The solution could have many elements, but we must start with two integrated parts:

1. **Building and sustaining an effective Project Management Function** (PMF): A PMF requires organizational recognition and acceptance (formality).

2. **Integration to Deliver Value** is crucial for establishing the PMF and **delivering consistent success**. This includes "vertical" and "horizontal" integrations.

Closing Remarks

We will keep the closing remarks brief:

*   **Project management can be a competitive advantage.**
*   **Project management can be indispensable for business results.**

However, we must transform project management, starting with the strategic aspects and formalizing the project management function, which is the role of the organization executives and board of directors.

CHAPTER 9

Project Management
As A Function

Introduction

It is time to propose our solution with the relevant attributes. However, first, let us emphasize a few definitions.

- **Formal Function**: An organizational function, like human resource, marketing, technology, and engineering, is recognized in the organizational system, hierarchy, and governance. A board of directors or organizational leadership formally set up these functions. This would be the case in organizations large enough to have departments, divisions, or organizational units (OU)[90]. This function is represented via an OU with a chief officer or executive leader.

---

[90] This would be the same thing as a Business Unit. However, we prefer an Organizational Unit since the organization could be a not-for-profit, non-governmental, or government organization, not a commercial business.

- **Project Management**: In the context of this book, project management refers to the 4PMs (Project, Program, Product[91], and Portfolio Management). In other words, the focus is not on managing a single project but on organizational project management.

- **Project Management Office (PMO)**: As discussed in an earlier chapter, a PMO is an organizational unit focusing on project management. Ideally, a PMO should oversee the project management function we propose here, and a few PMOs might have achieved what we propose. Unfortunately, reality and the current state have shown us that many (if not most) PMOs have not reached the maturity level to become genuine representatives of the entire project management function. Further, we still see confusion and chaos regarding the structure, mandates, value, and positions of PMOs within the organizational hierarchy.

Introductory Questions

What Is The Project Management Function?

Project management is not a formal organizational function in many organizations, meaning no project management division, section, or department exists.

---

[91] This is about the product development or delivery within the overall product management domain. We include here since projects and programs are often about producing a product.

This book is about formally establishing a project management function (PMF), represented by a project management division (PMD)[92].

We think it is essential that organizations understand, recognize, and accept project management as a function, including leadership, which would be via an executive-level position such as Chief Project Officer, Chief Project Management Officer, or Vice President of Project Management.

What Triggered This Proposal?

As you know, the primary trigger is minimizing project failure and enhancing organizations' ability to deliver on their strategies to maximize shareholder value. In Part A, we shared a few chapters about the current state of practice, including the challenges concerning project management and the C-Suite.

The following is additional information relevant to this question.

- Organizations have marketing projects, software projects, finance projects, and project management certifications, but no formality of the project management roles or the function. Many executives see project management as transactional work and not a permanent role. This is due to a lack of understanding of project management.
- It is essential to give these organizations and their executives the benefit of the doubt since project management is a relatively young domain. Project management is still not

---

[92] We use division generically to represent a department, division, or organizational (business) unit.

a common topic in colleges, and degree programs are rare, especially at the bachelor's level. As a result, some organizations are still discovering its value. Further, many executives could be coming from finance or MBA programs[93]. In other words, most of these executives did not study project management and probably never worked as project managers or directors.

A COUPLE OF STORIES

In one case, a workshop participant complained that her organization manages projects using PowerPoint.

She meant that the project management staff collect reports from their contractors or project management consultants, put the information in a presentation format, and share it with management. They do this without validation and, in some cases, even without proper understanding.

In another case, the project was to build a community of high-rise buildings. During construction, leadership decided to add a road in the middle of this new cluster of buildings, which is a considerable change with a massive impact. However, the general manager could not understand how "adding two lines on a drawing will have so much impact."

It is typical for large-scale and megaprojects to experience up to 40% in cost overruns (on average) (Merrow, 2011).

---

[93] It is worth noting that many leading MBA programs worldwide do not offer project management in their curriculum. Some might offer operations management but not project management.

- Some organizations working on capital projects have project management departments or divisions, so what we said here does not apply to them. However, other organizations (even those working on capital projects) do not have formal organizational project management functions or systems. If they do, a business unit for project management could be weak or limited to a few members who could be liaisons between the business and the contractors—more of a client's representative role. We have met professionals with less than five years of experience as project managers for a megaproject. We have worked with "clients' reps" who do not know how to read a schedule, understand earned value management, or even a project life cycle (see Stories textbox). Consequently, these individuals cannot manage a project effectively or make the right decisions.

The bottom line is that organizations have a choice:

1. One choice is to continue to be trapped in a cycle of doom due to outsourcing, over-dependence on contractors and consultants, going through the illusion of risk transfers through fixed-price and low-bid contracts, and preparing their blame messages. Blame project management, blame the project management consultants (PMCs), blame the contractors or the subcontractors until we have no one else to blame except Murphy.[94] In the end, continue the failure to achieve goals!
2. The other choice is to climb out of the cycle of doom and build and sustain the project management function (PMF).

---

[94] Once, a friend shared with us that the project manager and team were sacked on a billion-dollar outsourced project. They needed scapegoats. Murphy is a reference to Murphy's Law, "if anything that could go wrong, it will."

The PMF offers a robust organizational project management system, with a transparent organizational knowledge base and a significant focus on the people aspects—maturity, behaviors, and culture.

Why Do Organizations Need A Project Management Function?

We start with information from a megaprojects study. This quote is from Edward Merrow, founder of Independent Project Analysis (IPA), a company specializing in benchmarking projects.

"I believe that those charged with the education of business professionals . . . bear a good deal of the responsibility for the failures of business professionals in industrial firms" (Merrow, 2011). This statement is related to what we shared earlier about the absence of project management in universities and degrees.

Merrow also found that the organizations that used project management consultants (PMCs) were more likely to have failed projects[95] than those that did not. For example, PMC-led projects[96] experienced an average cost growth of 40%, which would make the project owners uncompetitive compared to their industry peers[97].

---

[95] In this context, failures are most often project management failures, such as cost overruns or schedule delays.

[96] These are the projects where the owner organization outsourced the project management to a specialized consultant/contractor.

[97] We often hear organizations might be better off focusing on their core business and outsourcing the project management function. If the organization does not have any project management expertise, then yes, that would make sense, especially if the need for project management is temporary. However, if the organization delivers assets/products through projects for years to come, it is most effective (as found by Merrow and others) in building the project management function.

It is important to stress that a PMC is a contractor with its own agenda and benefits. They still need support and guidance from the owner's organization. However, when owners' organizations lack project management competence and maturity, they fail to see the challenges and make the right decisions (refer to Stories text box from earlier).

We will emphasize what Merrow found. Although the information came from a megaprojects study, based on our decades of experience and working with numerous clients in various industries, we know it applies to other project types, regardless of industry, size, and complexity, and it is one of the primary triggers for this proposal.

THE EXCEPTIONS

We are saying that most organizations have not formalized the project management function. However, there are exceptions.

One exception we mentioned elsewhere is organizations working extensively on capital projects, like oil and gas. Project management divisions are standard in those situations, and we share case studies here.

The other exception is service providers, such as software development, engineering, technology, construction, and consultants. Many of these companies' work is on client projects. Therefore, it is natural to structure their service units as project management functions.

In other words, organizations need transformation founded on **the pillars of people, processes, and technology**. Therefore, organizations need project management as a core organizational function (see text box on exceptions[98]).

What Are the Benefits?

Organizations achieve a higher level of performance when they build the competence and capacity to lead their projects!

A project management function helps organizations centralize governance, standardization, adaptability, continual improvement, establish proper methodological processes, competency development, consistent performance, and many other factors. When the organization's governing body formally recognizes project management, it would reduce the silos effect and enhance collaboration across business units. Standardization[99] and knowledge sharing would help avoid recreating the wheel syndrome and offer practical methods with the right level of tailoring by competent teams.

A project management function (the 4PMs) significantly increases the chance of success, faster products to market, optimized capital deployment, and maximized shareholders' value. It is about impactful strategy implementation through project management.

---

[98] We acknowledge a colleague, Mr. Thomas Walenta (https://www.linkedin.com/in/thwalenta/), for reminding us about this fact.

[99] We realize that standardization is often linked to misconceptions such as "one-size-fits-all" or "set-in-stone." These misconceptions come from poor practices. Standardization must include room for innovation, adaptability, flexibility, and empowerment.

The most important reason for this transformation would be Vision Realized!

Can We Quantify The Benefits?

For emphasis, we will repeat some of the information we shared in the Executive Summary (Chapter 2).

Studies, including those by the University of California Berkeley (Ibbs & Reginato, 2000), Independent Project Analysis (Barshop, 2016), PMI® (The Project Management Institute®), and others, have demonstrated that organizations with higher levels of project management maturity and those that use proper methodological processes routinely achieve significant benefits. The benefits include increased speed to market, doubling the chance of achieving cost and schedule targets, increased profitability, higher competence and performance, and trending to lowering the cost of project management in the organization.

One colleague[100] (who reviewed this chapter) asked, *"What is your response to the difference in the study results from 2000 to 2024?"* This is a difficult question since we do not have many studies using the same analysis methods. Where we could get data, we have not noticed any notable difference in project success; the numbers fluctuate from one year to another.

---

[100] The colleague is Ms. Sandra Hoskins, also on the UrukPM board. Her LinkedIn profile is https://www.linkedin.com/in/sandrahoskins/.

The Project Management Function

Vision

The vision for this proposal is for organizations to establish project management as a core organizational function equivalent to the rest of the functions.

What It Is

Depending on the organization's size and structure, this could be an organizational unit, division, or department. It would be a centralized function with the power to set up the proper portfolio governance for the entire organization in collaboration with the executives and the other functions. Let us call this a project management division (PMD).

The project management division will be the "owner" of the project management function and responsible for establishing policies, procedures, guidelines, and methods for managing projects and programs. Part of the PMD will also include an integrated delivery unit (or multiple units if necessary) to manage some projects and programs (more on this when we discuss the structure).

What It Is Not

A project management function/division does not mean a centralized home for all project personnel or that this unit will manage all projects and programs. It is about centralized governance and standardization but in collaboration with other functions (see text box on Analogy).

ANALOGY

Please consider the following:

The finance function will set the rules for financial matters in organizations. The intent is to provide consistency for reporting and overseeing financial decisions. This will impact procurement, projects, operating expenses, and all other areas. Finance will not be involved in every transaction or decision; the appropriate division will manage those. However, finance will have the power to audit.

The human resources function will operate similarly. They will set the rules for recruiting, training, promotions, and general people management, which other divisions will have to comply with.

People

For many reasons, it is impractical for the PMD to house everyone working on projects. This is vital to understand since many professionals would work more effectively from their divisions and areas of expertise. They need to maintain their domain of expertise. If any of these resources decide to make project management their career choice, it is possible to reassign them to the PMD.

A relevant note

We could not find research that presents us with the percentage of employees within an organization who work on projects or in a project management role. A sizable percentage of people might be working on projects (depending on the type of organization).

However, if we zoom in on those in project management roles, one reference indicates that up to 10% is possible. In one industrial conglomerate, we know that internal project management resources comprise about 5%, and this number excludes external contractors working on projects.

One study that we found[101] showed the degree of projectification (people working on projects) in different countries. The study stated, "Projectification is 34.7% in Germany, 32.6% in Norway, and 27.7% in Iceland." This was per 2013-2014 data (Schoper, Wald, Ingason, & Fridgeirsson, 2018). In other words, it was about one-third of the workforce. This rate was trending upward from earlier years.

Although about one-third might work on projects, not everyone will be part of the PMD. The PMD will house the portfolio management people, subject matter experts, and some project management personnel directly involved in projects (career project managers). Others will stay within their divisions and departments.

Further, the PMD will help all personnel working on projects through formal leadership and competency development programs, including shadowing, coaching, and mentoring. An effective learning and development program should start by categorizing people into groups, such as technical team members, project management team members, project and program managers, and portfolio management staff, and must include senior managers and executives. Then, the PMD would offer awareness sessions, orientations, or in-depth training appropriate for each group.

---

[101]   Shared by a colleague, Mr. Thomas Walenta (https://www.linkedin.com/in/thwalenta/).

Mandate

The following are some of the areas that should be under the mandate of the project management division (also see Structure below). We are only listing the most significant items. Please refer to the next chapter for more details.

- Oversee the project management function for the entire organization. This would include supporting the formulation of the strategy and offering the link between formulation and implementation. Further, manage the entire portfolio (with the proper delegation where needed; *see Analogy text box*). The value of this mandate is to enhance the strategy formulation process with project insights. Also, it provides the needed consistency across the different divisions regarding delivery, reporting, and governance.
- Build and sustain the organizational project management system, including a suite of tailored methods suitable for the organization's diverse project types. The value here is the level of standardization that would lead to a higher level of maturity and a better ability to deal with change.
- Lead the leadership and competency development of all people involved or affected by projects, up to the executive level. People's competency is directly related to organizational processes, not generic and external guides.
- For an effective and accountable project management function, the PMD must be able to review and audit the other functions' projects to identify gaps in practice and proactively provide the necessary support. Mature organizations understand the differences between constructive reviews

and the act of audit for policing to find the guilty or who to blame.

Leadership

As mentioned earlier, we think it is essential to establish strong leadership through an executive-level position such as Chief Project Officer, Chief Project Management Officer, or Vice President of Project Management.

This would end the challenge faced by PMOs today in continuing to ask for a seat at the table. However, this is not about a seat or ego; it is for this executive position to be an influential contributor to the organization's strategic direction and to ensure that project management can be indispensable for organizational success.

A Working Example

Here is an example (marketing function):

- Initially[102], the project management division would work with marketing to create the processes and tailored methods for the marketing projects and train the marketing project personnel (managers and team members).
- Then, marketing personnel could manage their day-to-day projects, seeking support from the PMD when necessary.
- Further, the PMD can access the marketing project reports and performance and review and analyze them to identify gaps and areas for improvement.

[102] Upon forming the project management division and when they start working on standardization.

The above would apply to human resources, finance, information technology, and other functions.

OPERATIONS VERSUS PROJECTS

Most organizational functions are operational in nature. This means their day-to-day would typically repeat and follow standard operating processes. For example, in marketing, posting on social media or sending email messages are mostly operational activities that follow the established guidelines.

On the other hand, each of these departments (functions) could have projects. By definition, a project would be about creating something or a notable change to an existing system. Staying with marketing, developing a new website could be treated as a project. A marketing campaign for a new product would benefit from project management thinking.

A Possible Structure

The following is a possible structure with a brief explanation. It is a high-level view, and reviewing this with the Mandate would be helpful. In large organizations, the PM Division would have these areas as departments where each department could have smaller units.

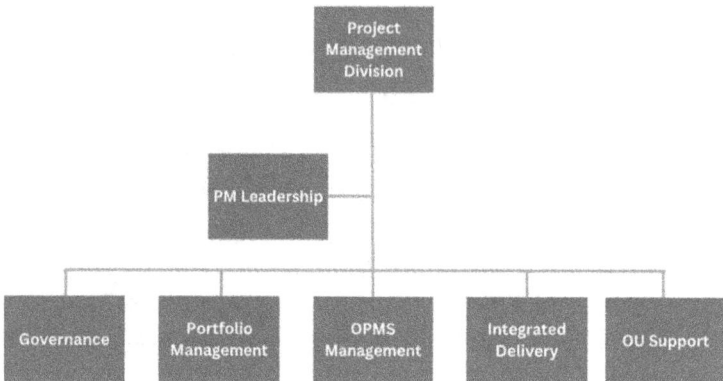

Figure No 9.1: The Envisioned Project Management Division

- **PM Leadership**: We show PM Leadership as an "assistant" box. This is optional since the people here could be part of the lower-level units. However, in large organizations, this could be a valuable concept. The intent is that this will be for the top, most senior advisors/experts for various project management roles, such as risk, cost, scheduling, or other experts.

  For example, in one petrochemical company with 10,000+ employees, there would be one chief project manager, one chief cost engineer, and the same for other project management roles. These would be like the Gurus and process owners of the given project management area. It is important to stress that the number of experts and their focus areas will depend on the industry, and what works for industrial companies will be different than the needs of technology companies or financial institutions.

  Further, these top experts do not have operational roles (not managing a unit). Due to the professional ladder, they are classified as senior managers or executives regarding benefits and compensation (*see Dual Ladders text box*).

DUAL LADDERS

In many organizations, people can only rise in rank if they follow a management ladder. Therefore, they are not motivated to stay in a technical role. The consequence would be a shift to management, which could cause them to rise to their level of incompetence. Alternatively, they stay stuck in lower-level technical roles.

On the other hand, some organizations have dual ladders. In addition to the management ladder, they have a professional ladder. Such a practice allows those with excellent technical skills to continue the professional ladder and become mentors and top experts as process owners of the given area. To maintain the motivation, these leaders will be compensated at the managers rank without the headaches of management, where they could fail.

- **Governance**: This unit within the PMD is responsible for the overall governance[103] of the portfolio, programs, and projects. It could include the team responsible for audits, reviews, and compliance with organizational systems and laws, if applicable.

---

[103] Governance is the framework of rules, practices, and processes by which an organization is directed and controlled. It encompasses the systems of accountability, decision-making, and oversight that ensure the organization's activities are aligned with its goals, ethical standards, and regulatory requirements.

- **Portfolio Management**: This unit would oversee the entire portfolio. It would participate in the strategy formulation exercise and help translate it into change initiatives, programs, and projects. This unit will also monitor and ensure real-time reporting through the executive dashboards. This unit might resemble the role of an enterprise PMO.

- **Organizational Project Management System**: This team is responsible for building the organizational project management system and methods in collaboration with the other functions. Once the OPMS is ready, the need shifts to enhancement based on feedback and research. This is like a PMO that implements an organizational project management system.

Suppose project management learning and development and career management are not separate units within the PMD. In that case, this OPMS unit oversees this work, which is an excellent fit for embodying the pillars of people, processes, and technology. It is also easier to link professional and competency development to the established processes.

Further, the top experts are housed here if the PM Leadership is not a separate unit.

In other words, this unit is like the research and development unit, researching, developing, and enhancing processes and methods, leading and developing people, and providing process leadership and ownership.

- **Integrated Delivery**: This unit executes the programs and projects led by the central unit and houses the project management personnel (see case studies later). The personnel in this unit are likely to be the people who have chosen project management as a career choice and would include program and project managers and other project management specialists.

- **Organizational Units (OU) Support**: If necessary, we can include a few resources in this unit to support the project management teams in the various functions. It is possible that some functions (other organizational units) might not have expertise in change or risk management and other project management topics, and they would need help.

Open Questions and Concerns

Please note that the next chapter, Visualizing the Future, will elaborate on how this project management division will operate. Here, we include some of the questions we received when presenting this proposed envisioned future.

Would This New Division Require Additional Resources?

The shared structure and mandates might give the impression that the organization implementing a project management division will need an army of additional resources, significantly increasing the overhead. This should not be the case.

First, many resources in the project management leadership and OPMS units can actively work on the various organizational projects, programs, and portfolios. Those resources and roles are necessary in all cases unless they are outsourced.

Also, many of these resources might already exist in the various organizational units. Therefore, all that is required is to reassign some of them to the PMD (see Case Study 1 at the end of this chapter for a relevant example).

Further, a higher level of project management maturity, with established systems and methods, would notably increase the efficiency and effectiveness of the various teams. This improvement is achieved since team members are not constantly looking to recreate the wheel and can allocate additional time to be proactive and minimize errors and wasting time on rework. This is evident in the University of California Berkeley study that shows project management costs drop once achieving stage 3 of project management maturity (Ibbs & Reginato, 2000).

However, in terms of total transparency, the program management team, which could include external consultants, is needed in the initial months of implementing this transformation program. The organization must also allocate time for training and development. Therefore, the overall project management cost will increase initially but drop later (as shown in the Berkeley study).

Finally, in large organizations, it is possible to require a few additional people, such as project management leaders, who might own the various processes. However, these also function as internal consultants and contribute significant value to projects and teams, including training, mentoring, and coaching.

Is This Not The Same as a PMO?

It might appear that this is the same as a PMO. If it is, it would be a rare case[104] where a PMO is formally recognized as a core organizational function, but for some reason or another, it is still called a PMO. However, in most cases, this is different from a PMO, and depending on the type of PMO, the difference could be massive. We are not aware of any PMO that fully aligns with this vision. Most PMOs cover only parts of this vision.

For example:

- A PMO within a department is only responsible for projects within that department (often, it is IT).
- A cPMO or ePMO might be involved in decisions about projects. It is also possible that these PMOs might be involved with strategy formulation or portfolio management. However, these PMOs will not be involved in project delivery.
- Some PMOs might implement the organizational project management system, but many do not.
- Some PMOs might be responsible for project delivery, but this is not true for most PMOs.
- Further, within the same organization, there could be more than one PMO, each with a different mandate, which would add to the fragmentation and often miss the synergies and consistency across the organization.

---

[104] My colleague, Mr. Thomas Walenta (https://www.linkedin.com/in/thwalenta/) shared that he ran such a PMO from 1995 to 2000 for an insurance company.

A quick exercise:

If your organization already has a PMO, create a matrix with one column for it and note everything it does now. Then, add a column for the PMD, as we outlined here. Are there differences or gaps?

Here is a sample comparison to help you get started. We are not including everything, and our answers are tentative since we do not know your situation.

Table 1: Comparing Different PMOs to the Project Management Division (PMD)

Work/Scope	Supportive	Department[105]	Corporate	PMD
Project Reports	Yes	Yes	No	Yes
Portfolio Reports	Maybe	Maybe	Yes	Yes
Career Management	Maybe	No	No	Yes
Professional Development	Maybe	Maybe	No	Yes
OPM System	No	Maybe	No	Yes
PM Methods	No	Maybe	No	Yes
Project Selection	No	No	Yes	Yes
Project Delivery	No	Maybe	No	Yes
Expert Support	Maybe	Maybe	No	Yes
Support Strategy Formulation	No	No	Yes	Yes
Centralized Resource Management	No	No	Maybe	Yes

Further, we want to emphasize that in most cases, a single executive might decide to set up a PMO, and the same executive or her replacement could dismantle the PMO. However, a project

---

[105] Anything in the column would be limited to one department or division.

management organizational unit is typically established by a board of directors' decision and included in the organization's governance and hierarchy.

Therefore, we are proposing elevating the PMO in the organizational hierarchy.

Does This Mean That The PMD Will Manage All Projects?

No!

Please refer to the earlier section to clarify the mandate and working example.

Does This Proposal Not Lead To Overlaps In The C-Suite?

At the C-Suite, would the Chief Project Officer (CPO) not overlap with the Chief Strategy Officer (CSO), the Chief Operating Officer (COO), or other executives? Is it not possible to duplicate effort?

This should not be the case.

With proper planning and governance when establishing the project management division, management can ensure proper delineation of responsibilities. For example, when formulating the strategy, the CSO would lead the effort, supported by the CPO and the other executives. Once approved, the CPO translates the formulated strategy for execution through projects and programs in collaboration with the other executives. Further, the CPO has insight into capacity, competencies, feasibility, etc., to help refine the strategy with the CSO.

Therefore, this would be a partnership!

This concept is like the CFO's responsibility for the organization's finances in collaboration with the other executives. The same is true for the other functions and executives.

What Are The Risks And Rewards?

What are the risks and rewards of this proposal?

When the organization is ready to proceed with this transformation, it should treat it like a strategic program, including the proper business case, feasibility study, understanding of the organizational culture, identification of supporters and blockers, and identification of risks. Our next book, **Building the Project Management Function**, would be a program guide (a playbook) that provides the transformation team with the necessary details to ensure success.

However, as with any strategic transformation initiative, the primary risk is resistance to change due to fear of the impact and uncertainty. Also, it is possible to have fears and concerns about leaders sharing authority or responsibility. Further, some organizational units might view the PMD as an enforcement agency. Therefore, the proper risk assessment will depend highly on the organization's culture and preparedness. The program approach we propose helps minimize the resistance.

For the rewards, please refer to the earlier chapters and sections regarding performance improvement, eliminating pain points, and more outstanding achievements for shareholders and personnel.

Are There Any Other Case Studies?[106]

One might ask: *"You shared case studies from industrial companies. We are a financial institution, a medical company, a technology company, a not-for-profit organization, or a government entity. How would this work for us?*

Unfortunately, because this is a relatively non-conventional idea, we do not have case studies showing the full implementation of every component of this proposal. We know some service providers and consultants might have adopted a similar model for their personnel working on client projects. However, let us consider PMOs, the concept closest to our proposal.

Years ago, some PMOs failed quickly. Today, we are still facing challenges with PMOs; however, if we consider the positives, according to PM Solutions and Statista, about 70-80% of companies today have PMOs, which is a sign of acceptance and value. Like projects, organizations can work toward success, and with competence and maturity, they can achieve it.

How About The Implementation?

How long would this transformation take?

Well, it depends on your starting point.

It could be months if you are in a situation where a PMO exists and it is doing well.

---

[106] Other than the ones we share in the next section of this chapter.

However (for organizations with absent or weak project management systems), this proposed state is like any transformation initiative and takes time. A longer timeframe is necessary to gradually acquire most of the change's benefits. However, organizations can start achieving benefits soon after initiating the transformation and will continue to improve.

PROGRAM APPROACH

It is critical to understand that organizations interested in adopting this proposal should do so with great agility (what we call a program approach). In other words, they should be implemented gradually, incrementally, and iteratively. We address this point later in this chapter, but we felt it necessary to touch on it now since this mandate might seem overwhelming.

Should we implement everything immediately?

Yes, if you want to fail quickly, which we do not think is wise.

Significant changes and transformations require a slow but steady process. We believe that such a change requires a program management approach (*see text box*), where the program is subdivided into numerous small projects and embraces great agility. In other words, subdivide the work into chunks, analyze, design, and implement each chunk as a project, an increment. Then, roll it out, collect feedback, and improve. While the teams are working on the new change from the first project, the transformation team will work on the next increment, where they will analyze, design, and implement. Repeat the cycle until complete transformation and assimilation.

A program approach will minimize the effect of the primary risk, the resistance to change. If done in small increments, new thinking will be easier to assimilate and accept. This is the primary focus of our next book, **Successful Transformation**.

Does This Proposal Lead To Replacing What Exists?

An excellent transformation team will not scrap what exists and build from scratch. If they do, you have an ego-centric team unwilling to take the time to respect what exists. Such a team might also introduce copy-paste solutions from different contexts and clients, which can be counterproductive.

A good transformation team recognizes that many organizations could already have elements of this system in place, even valuable undocumented practices. Therefore, the team will assess what exists, keep those components working well, improve what could be improved, scrap what does not work, and add new concepts or processes that do not yet exist.

How About The Role Of The CPO?

The role of the Chief Project Officer (CPO) is critical. However, delegating this role to existing C-suite individuals as champions is a common practice. The challenge is that these C-suite executives might not have enough expertise. As a result, they might hire consultants or a PMO director. They might lack a fundamental understanding of a true CPO role and objective. It is like the mindset that anyone can run a project.[107] The CPO must be a dedicated role equal to other C-suite roles and must lead the project management division and function.

Some practitioners have also raised the point that the CPO role is the same as the Chief Operating Officer (COO). In a special context, this might be true. However, in most cases, these are two distinct roles, each with a mandate. Then, there must be some overlap. We answered this point earlier.

Real World Examples

Case Study 1

An industrial company operating globally had a few business units (BUs) organized along their product lines. Each BU had a project management division. However, this led to fragmentation, where each PMD operated independently and had limited coordination. Further, the organization still had the traditional silos between the distinct functions and project management. Another level of complication was the global reach.[108]

It is worth noting that this company participated in benchmarking studies, and it ranked about average among its peers. That was a shock (almost an insult) since management expected to be among the leaders. Consequently, this company embarked on a transformation initiative in response to the benchmarking results and other factors.

---

[107] A colleague, Dr. Waffa Adam raised this point during her review. Here is her LinkedIn Profile: https://www.linkedin.com/in/waffa-adam-p-813a701/.

[108] This was before the days of smart phones and online communication platforms. So, communication was limited to emails or travel for a face-to-face.

- **Step 1**: The first step was to create a business unit (BU) for Engineering and Project Management, headed by a Vice President. This BU had engineering and project management divisions, each led by a general manager.

- **Step 2**: The PM Division structure included a central group responsible for overseeing the project management function and included the project management leadership (the experts for each area). Their mandate included ownership of the project management system, career management, advisory, and other duties. One execution role was for the core unit to lead the front-end planning for any project worth over $50 million and maintain oversight.

- **Step 3**: They formed five project management departments in various locations worldwide, where they had many facilities to support. This was necessary to ensure project management was close to operations to build relations and offer effective support. Each department had the autonomy to handle the projects within its geographic area. These projects were often within or next to operating facilities and typically cost $1 to $50 million. If they have a project much more extensive than this, then the central team will take over.

- **Step 4**: Moved all project management personnel from the previous structure (the different product business units) into these departments and the core unit.

This change effectively contributed to project performance, cross-learning, and other benefits. This organization also embraced the dual ladder concept and had a project management professional ladder. It also had an internal project management credential with clear criteria for this recognition.

Case Study 2

This was also an industrial company operating globally and had a **project management business** unit led by a vice president and four permanent departments.

- One department was a central unit that functioned like a portfolio management office and included front-end planning for all large-scale and megaprojects. This department also included an estimating group and a best practices group.
- The three other departments were spread geographically, each responsible for a set of facilities within their geographic region.
- In addition to the above, every time the organization considered a megaproject, they formed a dedicated department for this new business initiative. Although these were called departments, they functioned like a giant, extended project team. The extended project team would follow a projectized organization model. These new departments were under the oversight of the project management business unit and followed the established organizational project management systems.

It is worth noting that this was one of the few industrial organizations in the region with this structure. This organization's internal teams led most of its worldwide projects, whereas other companies depended on project management consultants (PMCs). We shared earlier the benchmarking research by Edward Merrow, which states that organizations with internal management do better than those outsourced to PMCs. Unfortunately, this organization did not embrace the dual ladder concept.

Closing Remarks

In this book, we wanted to limit the discussions to the core ideas, make a case for change, and share the envisioned future. The remaining chapters will build on the core concept and elaborate further on what is necessary for the transformation. This book would function as the business case for this transformational initiative. It is a starting point on an exciting journey.

Please note that to the best of our knowledge, we have not seen the entirety of our proposal in the community. Despite this fact (partial system), many organizations achieved significant benefits. **Therefore, can you imagine the added benefits resulting from the significant synergies that a centralized project management division will bring?**

CHAPTER 10

Visualize the Future

Introduction

This chapter supplements the previous one and is core to our proposed vision. We address various areas of the mandate to clarify how this project management division (PMD) will operate. It is to visualize the future of work. However, please note the following:

Is your organizational culture pulling you DOWN or lifting you UP?

The attached image provides us with the three areas of interest within organizations. These include corporate processes (including strategy formulation), business and technical processes (operations), and organizational project management processes (OPMS).

Important Clarifications

Operations versus Projects

First, we must clarify that organizations work through operations and projects (in addition to their corporate processes). Typical operations include marketing, sales, engineering, accounting, and other work that should happen per the standard operating procedures. Operations management is outside the scope of our book.

Our focus is on projects and project management. Please remember that this is in the context of the 4PMs (project, program, product, and portfolio management). So, when we say our focus is on projects, it automatically means programs and all aspects of organizational project management.

Project Management Division Role

With the first clarification noted, the second point to clarify is our proposal that the project management division will have a lead role in the organization. We will explain the role of the division's various units.

Partnership

As outlined in the previous chapter, the CPO role should be in partnership with the CSO and other executives. The PMD must also collaborate with all other organizational units to ensure optimal alignment.

Strategy Formulation

In organizations with a Chief Strategy Officer (CSO), that position leads the development of the organizational strategy and its updates. However, this is never a single-person or strategy office job. The CSO leads but must collaborate with all other executives. Creating a strategy requires significant input from the organization (internal factors) and understanding the external factors, drivers, challenges, and opportunities. This book is not a guide to formulating strategy, so we limit the discussion to the role of the Chief Project Officer (CPO) and the project management division in the strategy formulation effort.

How can the project management division contribute to strategy formulation?

The following is one example:

A well-structured and functioning project management division has much information about past and ongoing projects, including their performance, lessons, and other insights. With proper resource allocation and monitoring projects' work, the PMD knows resource utilization and organizational capacity. They know about lessons learned and the factors contributing to success or causing failure.

Therefore, as the executive committee is working on a new strategic plan, they must know the organization's internal capacity to take on more work and whether they have the necessary competence.

THE EXCEPTIONS

Once, we met with a senior manager from a global airline who was tasked with establishing a PMO. To start his work, he tried to find information about the number of ongoing or past projects. He could not find anything, so he spent weeks talking to every division to collect information about the ongoing projects.

The result was a list of hundreds of projects. He told me, "Every idea became a project in this organization. There is no screening or coordination."

It was clear that this organization did not have a project management system, project tracking, or archives. What are the consequences of such practice?

There are many consequences, and the following is one example.

When a company considers new priority projects, it cannot find the resources to manage or do the work; everyone is busy on projects (some were low priority). Therefore, they must cancel some projects to push the high-priority projects. Alternatively, they can postpone the high-priority work.

Can you imagine the level of lost efforts and wasted resources that had already occurred on those canceled projects?

For example, a company wants to adopt AI (Artificial Intelligence) transformation. Internal information should be able to determine whether the organization has that competence; if not, it needs to develop that competency or hire experts.

Another example would be when an organization wants to offer a new service or product. The PMD can help by sharing internal knowledge and lessons from past work, which could help decide whether the organization is ready to take on this new service or product now or should delay it.

If the PMD does not exist, then the organizational knowledge base might be spread among many divisions, and it is possible that the information is not organized or readily accessible (*see text box*). It is also possible that no one is keeping that information. However, a PMD with sound databases and archives should have all that information readily accessible, organized, and easy to use!

In an earlier chapter, we shared that while many organizations do not have problems formulating strategies, they face problems in implementation. Now, reflect on what we just wrote:

- Without that internal knowledge (managed by the PMD), is the formulated strategy likely to have gaps or weaknesses, if not faulty?
- We know the PMD cannot eliminate all gaps. However, does the PMD help minimize problems due to the history, insights, and facts and avoid assumptions?

Strategy Implementation

Now that we have a strategy and a strategic plan, what can the PMD offer?

What we describe below is part of the portfolio management unit's mandate.

Step 1

The first action is to split the various strategic goals into sub-portfolios,[109] programs,[110] and projects.[111]

This work must be done in collaboration with the other executives since they are the owners/sponsors of these change initiatives. For example, the human resource function owns and sponsors transforming an organization's recruitment practice, with PMD leading the project or program to deliver the outcome. In other words, HR is the internal customer, and the PMD would be the implementation agency.[112]

---

[109] We subscribe to the view that each organization has one portfolio that includes all sub-portfolios, programs, projects, and other operational work. The sub-portfolios would be for each organizational unit.

[110] Often, long-term goals and change initiatives are best treated like programs, not projects. Programs are best for leading an initiative where there is some ambiguity and where the work might be best handled through a few projects over an extended period.

[111] Projects are also change initiatives. If the strategic plan includes a change with clear objectives and limited ambiguity, then a project could be a choice instead of a program.

[112] In a later chapter, we share the Value Delivery Methodology.

Step 2

The following action is to develop rough plans for the various programs and projects. These plans are conceptual and should include the approximate cost and duration, expected starting date, critical deadlines, if any, and the required resources (people and physical), preferably by type. Tabulating this information with resource management provides many insights, including potential resource shortages (or excesses). These projects and programs are future work, a long-term backlog (the innovation or projects pipeline). When the organization is ready to proceed with one of these projects, it can do so by starting to follow the proper methodology.

Step 3

It is time to prioritize the projects' backlog. Depending on the organization's resources and the importance and urgency of the change initiatives, and the adopted selection criteria, the PMD (with other divisions) can prioritize the various initiatives.

We must emphasize that Steps 2 and 3 directly influence each other, and some iterations are required.

What Is Next?

What is next is the core of the project management division's operation. It would include:

- Portfolio management, which we will discuss next.
- Integrated delivery is a subject we will mention later in this chapter, with details in another chapter.

- There is a need to monitor the various conditions that affect the work and determine the need for updates due to emergent trends and performance.

Portfolio Management

The project management division should have different units,[113] as outlined in the structure in the previous chapter. Portfolio Management is one of those units.

What is the role of portfolio management?

A significant part of the mandate would be:

- Participate in the strategy formulation and offer the link between formulation and implementation.
- Convert the formulated strategy into change initiatives, programs, and projects.
- Continue to monitor the projects and programs list and update it where necessary.

In addition to the above, here are some other mandates.

- House the portfolio management team.
- Oversee the project management function for the entire organization.
- Function in an advisory capacity to the executive committee and the board of directors.

---

[113] If this implies a significant additional overhead, please refer to the previous chapter where we addressed this concern.

- Manage the entire portfolio (with the proper delegation where needed).
- Own the organization's projects archive.
- Monitor the numerous performance metrics and look for red flags.
- Analyze the entire system or specific components.

Governance

It is possible to position this unit under the portfolio management unit. However, in large organizations, it might be helpful to keep them separate since governance would involve overseeing the entire project management division and its various units. For example, for an effective and accountable project management function, the PMD must be able to review and audit the other functions' projects. This would be part of the mandate of the governance unit.

To fully understand governance at the organization, portfolio, or project levels, additional coverage is required, which is outside the scope of this book.

Organizational Project Management System Management

The organizational project management system (OPMS) is a must for the project management division and should be for every project management office. Without it, there will be no processes, structure, or consistency, and we will recreate the wheel with every new project or program.

We often discuss the three pillars of successful project management: people, processes, and technology. The OPMS is the processes[114] pillar. Once the processes (OPMS) are in place, we can train and develop the people (team members, managers, and executives) according to the processes in place.

If not separated, this OPMS unit could include the learning, development, and career management team. This team will use the OPMS (processes) to establish the competency baseline for all project-related roles (from team members to executives). Then, it will design a professional development program per the competency baseline.

Therefore, this unit mandate includes:

- Build the organizational project management system.
- Sustain the OPMS with continual improvement.
- Participate in conferences and conduct research and development for continual improvement.
- Assess project management trends and consider the implementation of valuable insights.
- Share knowledge with the project management community.
- Establish a suite of tailored methods suitable for the diverse types of projects in the organization.
- Lead the leadership and competency development of all people involved or affected by projects, up to the executive level.
- Possibly conduct training and lead workshops.

---

[114] In this context, processes represent governance, policies, guidelines, procedures, and methods.

- Along with portfolio management, this unit might also serve in an advisory capacity.
- Finally, if PM Leadership is not a separate unit, OPMS Management will be a good home.

It is important to emphasize that when the PMD is new, a team is needed to build the processes, methods, and systems for the 4PMs. This team can stay small and build the OPMS gradually (iteratively and incrementally). Depending on the level of project management within the organization, this team could consist of internal experts, but it is possible to include external resources. Once the OPMS is established, maintaining it becomes part of the routine project management operations.

Integrated Delivery

In an earlier chapter, we shared case studies where integrated delivery could involve multiple departments if the organization is massive. This unit (or multiple units) would house the project management personnel involved. It could include an estimating and budgeting team separated from the projects to avoid conflict of interest.[115] Otherwise, this unit will include the various project teams leading projects not typically handled in other divisions and organizational units.

---

[115] This would be a topic for the Transforming Project Management book. However, we can mention here that it would be beneficial if the organization have the cost estimating and initial scheduling performed by a unit that does not fall under the control of the project managers. We realize that this goes against current thinking since the preference is for the project manager to lead or do the cost estimates.

We must emphasize a critical concept here. This unit will house the project management personnel, those working on projects as project management teams, including program and project managers, project control, quality, risk, procurement, and other roles. These roles do not include the technical team members such as software developers, engineers, and other resources that would be conducting the technical work.[116] Those technical people are from all other functions and borrowed or assigned to projects on a part- or full-time basis. When their work is completed, they return to their units or could be assigned to other projects. This is known as a matrix organization[117] (often a strong matrix).

Organizational Unit Support

Since the various organizational units can handle many projects, their project managers might often require help from specialists, such as risk, change, procurement, or scheduling experts. Therefore, an OU Support unit is established if the volume of work justifies the need for a separate unit. Otherwise, the integrated delivery unit can provide the support.

Closing Remarks

We cannot cover all the activities and actions a project management division can handle. However, we provided a reasonable explanation to help readers visualize this department's work. Obviously, some organizations will need all the above and more. Other organizations can function well with some of these units. Therefore, it is essential

---

[116] Here is a relevant video: https://youtu.be/VeGUxQpgtUs.

[117] For more information about project's organizational structures, please refer to the previous link.

to understand that the one-size-fits-all concept does not work here. Each PMD must comply with the organization's industry, domain, type of work, culture, and level of maturity.

For example, in the case studies shared in the previous chapter, one organization had a best practices team. Another organization had a dual ladder, whereas another did not offer the option of a professional ladder. One organization had an internal certification program and did not care about certification programs by project management associations, while another followed the associations' offerings. One organization had a mandatory cross-functional program where a project management person must work in different project management roles for at least one to two years in each assignment. In one case, those assignments could be outside project management.

A final reminder: the size of the PMD (or Organizational Unit) varies greatly and directly depends on the size of the organization, the number of projects, the size of the capital program, and many other factors. For example, the portfolio management unit could be a couple of people or ten, which applies to all other units. Unfortunately, we do not have many studies that can help determine the number of people. However, based on experience, 5-10% of the employee count could be a rough indicator. However, as mentioned earlier, the study on projectification (Schoper, Wald, Ingason, & Fridgeirsson, 2018) stated that about one-third of the employees could be working on projects. However, as outlined in this book, most of those will not belong to the PMD.

CHAPTER 11

Integrations To Deliver Value

Introduction

We have outlined that one of the problems facing the project management community in organizations is the fragmentation of the project management practice. This is a significant contributor to project failure and challenges. In this chapter, we briefly address the indicators of fragmentation and offer our concept of **Integrations to Deliver Value!**

Defining Value

In the project management community, we often discuss project delivery, product delivery, and output delivery. Why are we using the term value delivery?

Some suggest that projects do not deliver value; they deliver the output, which provides the capabilities to generate value. They will debate the differences between output and outcome. We think this is a fragmentation mindset.

Yes, we agree that for a project to deliver a clinic (product), the building will not generate revenue (value). However, the owner did not launch this project unless they expected it to generate value (revenue, profit, or community service if not-for-profit). Therefore, the objective is to deliver value, not products.[118]

Project-owner organizations must realize that projects (and programs) are investments; hence, they must think of value rather than output. This is a distinct perspective from vendors, contractors, or consultants, whose mandates are often limited to delivering an output (product or service).

Indicators of Fragmentation

As a reminder, what are some of the indicators of this fragmentation?

- Planning projects and programs as stand-alone initiatives, often without coordinating with portfolio management.

  For example, without resource planning for the organization (portfolio level), each project team develops its plan assuming that specific resources are available. What happens if another project makes the same assumption for the same resources? If the organization does not have centralized resource planning,[119] potential conflicts could arise. Further, this situation is often overlooked if no processes require integration (coordination) between project and portfolio

---

[118] Three short videos about this subject (total of six minutes): https://youtu.be/nlsrQ36qJog, https://youtu.be/9gOOkRr1oYo, and https://youtu.be/K2d2WI2Czrk.

[119] In the previous chapter, we stressed that this would be essential for supporting the strategy formulation and implementation.

levels, or between projects and the rest of the organizational units that provide those resources. Consequently, the teams will discover resource problems during the implementation, which might lead to delays and cost overruns.

- Lack of ongoing communication between project management and the other functions. This is a sign of the silo effect with limited interfaces. The consequence here could be the lack of available resources when needed and the potential for scope creep and changes that could be disruptive.
- Absence of projects' and programs' prioritizations. As a result, resources might be locked when working on low-priority projects when there are high-priority projects that are pending or delayed.
- In some organizations, there are no sponsors for these projects, often leaving the project managers to fight for resources, sponsorship, and support.
- It is common practice to fall into siloed conditions, where a project moves from one silo to another without proper interfaces and handover, often without a single point of accountability (sponsor or project manager).

Example 1: Some capital projects might start with strategic or facilities planning, ideally[120] with a proper business case or feasibility. Once they define the product scope and high-level statement of work, they send the project to a front-end planning group. The front-end planning group would ideally perform proper planning, including cost estimates and initial

---

[120] We say "ideally" because in organizations with low project management maturity, it is common to skip some of these steps or complete these studies in a rush without the proper due diligence.

schedules, leading to final approval. With final approval, the project will be transferred to the implementation team. Hiring a project management consultant is necessary if the organization cannot manage such a project.[121] In either case, they must hire engineering and construction contractor(s), another interface. Finally, upon product completion, another handover to the operations team is required.

Example 2: We have a comparable situation on projects with software components. An organizational unit might need to implement a new system. They might do an initial scoping, which could include gaps if they do not consider all aspects. The requesting OU will likely not have a project manager or sponsor, at best, maybe a point of contact. Then, they hand over the project to IT for software development. IT might assign a technical lead (agile, scrum) or a project manager. However, in this case, the project manager focuses on building the product, not the entire project (in other words, this project manager is a stage manager). Another team might be working on operational readiness (another stage management). When all is done, there is a handover. Even if the work is done using agile development (iterative and incremental), it is possible to have many gaps.

In both examples, the silo effect is a form of fragmentation and lack of integration.

---

[121] In an earlier chapter, we mentioned that in one organization that reality was "We manage projects by PowerPoint." In other words, the project owner team is often playing a liaison role rather than leadership and management role.

There are many other examples, but we think the point is clear. Our proposed model advocates the idea of **Integrations to Deliver Value**, which requires vertical and horizontal integration.

Vertical Integration

Vertical integration is real-time integration between projects, programs, and portfolio management. This concept will have a positive effect on various parts of organizational project management and will be a significant contributor to success.

Benefits

Here are some of the benefits and value of vertical integration.

- Avoid the planning problems and duplication of resources mentioned earlier.
- Better coordination between projects, especially where there are interfaces.
- Enhanced collaboration between projects and programs.
- The benefits from the holistic management of the entire portfolio are primarily due to the ongoing coordination.
- Improved communication within the various levels of the organizational hierarchy.
- Real-time and transparent[122] reporting and synchronizing performance information from project and program to portfolio levels.

---

[122] This is possible with the use of technology (remember, people, processes, and technology). The Uruk Platform that UrukPM offers real-time and transparent performance reporting and executive dashboards.

The Components

The following briefly explains the various components in the shared illustration.

- **Project and Program Management**: We combine the two due to their similarities, especially since both should follow a methodological process that covers the change across the entire life cycle from ideation to operation. More on this later.

- **PM Actions**: This concept includes integrating the PM Actions. These actions include scope, cost, schedule, risks, change, quality, procurement, sustainability, team management, and similar focus areas. We must stress that we view project (and program management) as multi-dimensional work, including managing across the stages of the project life cycle and the various functions we listed.

- **Portfolio Management**: Please refer to the previous chapter for a brief description.

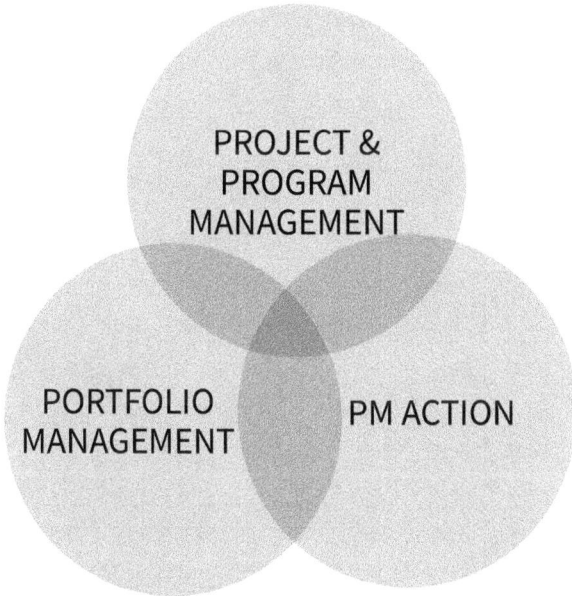

Figure No 11.1: Integrations to Deliver Value,
Vertical Integrations

Horizontal Integration

The term horizontal integration shifts the focus to leading a project (or a program) across the entire life cycle. The methodological process would require integrating project management with the rest of the organizational functions. The best way to explain this concept is to share the UrukPM Value Delivery Methodology, which we cover in the next chapter.

Closing Remarks

Once an organization decides to accept our proposal and form the project management function (division) or even stay with a project management office, it still needs to transform project management. We know that Integrations to Deliver Value are central to this transformation effort, especially for project owner organizations.

The value here is the cohesive management of the entire portfolio and linking project management to strategic planning and achieving the organization's purpose.

CHAPTER 12

Value Delivery

Introduction

In the previous chapter, we shared our value proposition for why we focus on value delivery instead of limiting our thinking to delivering a product or an output.

In this chapter, we discuss the concept of project management methodology and what is or is not a project management method. We also share the UrukPM **Value Delivery Methodology** as a manifestation of achieving horizontal integration.

Although this discussion might appear technical, we urge readers, especially senior managers and executives, to understand this concept to avoid many of the pitfalls we face, including fragmentations and hype.

We share a couple of statements that some may not consider politically correct. Today, many "experts" share posts to sell substandard or ineffective project management methodologies. Others are trying to sell methodologies, claiming these are by professional associations. Yet, most professional associations in project management do not offer project management methods. The problem is that many of these "experts" do not know the difference between method and methodology, process and method, technique and method, product and project work, etc. Some think project management is just a mindset or common sense.

Therefore, it is important to filter through this confusion.

Relevant Definitions

Value

Please refer to the previous chapter.[123]

Product

In the context of this book, a product can be software or hardware, a facility, or a service. Typically, a product has a life cycle. The image illustrates a typical product life cycle with five phases. An organization could have one or more projects and programs in each phase. However, to acquire the product (acquisition phase), a significant project is expected to take the product from ideation to initial operation. *Product management is outside the scope of this book.*

Project

Many professional associations have defined the term "project." The challenge is keeping the definition short and confined to one sentence. As a result, practitioners end up with different interpretations and

---

[123] We also have three short videos about this subject (a total of six minutes): https://youtu.be/nlsrQ36qJog, https://youtu.be/9gOOkRr1oYo, and https://youtu.be/K2d2WI2Czrk.

choose what suits them. For example, is construction work a project or a phase? Is software development work a project or a phase? Is cooking dinner for your family a project or a task? We can debate these various questions, which means trying to force a unique answer. We choose an alternative route: accepting that the definition is situational, hence the need to define it, at least in the context of this work. It is important to differentiate because this directly impacts how to manage the work.

Here are the general points we use to define a project:

- A project could be anything we create from scratch or a significant modification to an existing system, which would require substantial effort in development and delivery.
- A project has a specific product (output), objectives (outcome), defined timeline (schedule), budget, and various other parameters (resources, quality, risks, etc.).
- Delivering a product or service (output) requires an investment of time and money, and it must provide the capabilities to realize benefits (outcome).
- The project owner can verify and accept the output at completion and closeout but often cannot validate the outcome until months or years after the end of the physical work.

Product Life Cycle

Acquisition	Growth	Maturity	Decline	Withdrawal

End

Start

Within each of these phases, there could be one or more projects

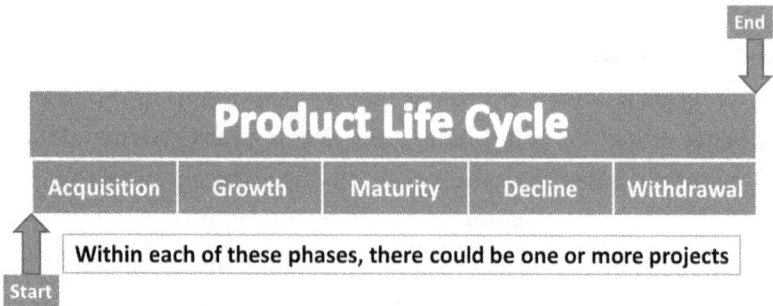

Figure No 12.1: A Typical Product Life Cycle

- Each project should follow a project life cycle.
- A project can be independent or part of a program. If it is part of a program, it must align with the program objective, which, in turn, must align with the organizational strategic direction. On the other hand, if the project is independent of a program, it must directly align with the organizational strategic direction.

What Is Not A Project?

These are the things that we do not consider a project.

- A routine task that can be accomplished in hours or days by one or more people
- A phase or stage of the project (a piece of it, usually along the project life cycle)
- A sub-project (also a piece of a project, which could be different parts or sections of a facility)
- A program or a portfolio.

So, is cooking dinner a project?

Theoretically, the answer could be yes if we limit the definition to output and ignore the other factors: outcome, objectives, significant effort to plan and implement, often a one-person job, etc. Anyway, it is up to you to define a project. However, if you do not want to be trivial, we advise you to look at the definition we presented.

Phase/Stage

A project has a life cycle, which consists of phases or stages.[124] Typically, each stage has a different focus, resulting in a unique output. For example, a feasibility stage involves conducting a feasibility study, with the output being a feasibility study report.

Method

See below.

Project Management Methods

Method versus Methodology

Method and methodology are often used interchangeably, but they have distinct meanings, especially in project management.

Method

A method is a specific procedure or technique for accomplishing a particular task or goal. It is a systematic way of doing something, often involving steps or actions. A method should encompass the

---

[124] In the project management community, we often use these two terms interchangeably. However, in the UrukPM model, we consider a stage as a subset of a phase.

entire process. Per the project management context, it should be from concept to closure, including the project life cycle, stages, and stage gates.

Methodology

On the other hand, a methodology is a comprehensive framework that includes a collection of methods, principles, and rules for managing a project.

In summary, while a method is a specific way of doing something, a methodology is a broader system that includes multiple methods and provides a structured approach to managing projects.

What Is A Project Management Method?

How do we define a project management method?

Is the definition limited to a project life cycle?

Are there other factors and considerations?

In general, we often use the term "method" to mean different things. Below are the two most common types.

Type 1

We often use the term project management method to mean doing something specific **within** a project. This is not about managing the entire project. For example:

- Earned Value Management (EVM) is a method (or technique) that can be used on projects.
- Critical Path Method (CPM) is also a method that can be used on projects.
- The same thinking applies to Agile. Agile "Methods" can be used on projects, usually in development.

However, just because we use the term method or technique on projects **does not mean the method is a project management method**, per our definition.

Type 2

With the above background and context, Type 2 is the definition we have adopted. **We depend on two principles to define a genuine project management method:**

- Since a project is a change initiative, a project management method must cover the entire value delivery life cycle, from the vision (ideation) to the final success assessment (post-initial operations). It must also integrate project management with the rest of the organizational functions.
- Due to the diversity of project management practice, the project management must align with the organizational culture and context. Therefore, the project management method must be adaptive and tailored to fit the project context.

Type 2 might be most suitable for project owner organizations. However, most of the principles and components also apply to service providers.

What Are The Components of a PM Method?

Here are the components of a project management method.[125] Please remember that this is a method for managing the entire project life cycle, not a technique/method we use for doing something within a project. The primary components are:

1. The foundation, a project life cycle (PLC),
2. The PLC has phases/stages,
3. We use the stage management processes to manage a stage,
4. Each stage has an output,
5. Each output must pass through an evaluation and decision point, a stage gate.
6. A method must also include the processes for managing the various applicable project management functions and actions, such as scope, cost, change, etc.

Further, the above core components must be customizable and adaptable (tailorable) to make the project management method suitable for a given context,[126] which leads to the development of a unique, tailored method.[127]

The Value of a Stage Gate Model

A core component of a project management method is the stage gates, and we know this concept intimidates many practitioners and executives. However, stage gates are vital for project success.

---

[125] A related video https://youtu.be/aArto1Mcaao
[126] The second principles we stressed earlier.
[127] This is the approach we are using to build the Uruk Platform, https://urukpm.com/

They are critical events throughout the project life cycle within this methodological approach.

Many practitioners outside capital projects have never heard of the stage gate model and claim they do not have it. It is rare for an organization to work on projects without stage gates. The only difference is that they might call them decision points (or something else), which could be as formal as stage gates. So, do not let this concept sideline or intimidate you.

Essential factors for the gates are:

- Competent project management practitioners agree that no one should work on a project without a product vision, an understanding of the stakeholders' expectations, and well-defined requirements. Each topic could be a stage output that goes through a stage gate for the stakeholders' review, alignment, and decision on whether to continue. If there are no gates, what prevents the team from moving from one stage to another without adequately completing the prior stage work? What would help the team avoid skipping a step without control points? Finally, what ensures the team implements the proper scope of work?
- The stage gates also play an essential role in organizational and project governance. The importance of such gates is especially pertinent as more and more projects are substantial investments. Therefore, project governance becomes a keystone of corporate governance.
- Another critical factor is determining the right project investment level for each stage. In other words, is the right amount of effort in place to balance the effectiveness and

efficiency of the application of project management? In each step, it is crucial to do just the required work necessary to meet the organizational requirements for the scope of the stage—no more, no less.

- Finally, please refer to Chapter 2, in which we stressed the value of this methodological model (in terms of speed to market and savings) and its direct contribution to project success.

The Uruk Model

The Uruk Model is how we have adopted and implemented the concept of horizontal integration. **It is the Uruk Value Delivery Methodology (VDM).**

A Common Practice

In an earlier chapter, we shared the concept of project management levels. The two most common levels our community members practice today are Level 2 and Level 3.

- Level 2 (a widespread practice in software and agile projects) is limited to managing the project's software development stage. In these situations, a service provider or the IT department would start with an already defined set of requirements and product backlog and work toward producing the product. This practice does not include the earlier stages as part of the project and ignores operational readiness and what happens post-handover. This is often the implementation stage in the illustration shown below.

- Level 3 is broader and aligns with the concept that a project starts with a charter and ends with the handover of the output. In this case, the approach ignores a project's critical discovery phase, operational readiness stages, and what happens post-handover. In the illustration, this is what we label the Project Life Cycle.

The Value Delivery Methodology

The following illustration is a typical method that aligns with this approach: Level 5[128] in our model.

Please remember, this is an example. A project life cycle could be four stages or ten. We could combine stages or split stages. Although the image shows most stages as sequential, they do have some overlaps, and in some cases, the overlap can be significant. One can also see some parallel stages. Further, the name of every stage could vary from one domain to another.[129]

We can imagine some practitioners thinking this is a waterfall, but it is not. This methodology is a real-world, practical, agile model.[130] Let us clarify:

---

[128] For a discussion on leading projects per the different levels, please refer to this webinar recording: https://youtu.be/rC4quAaswLA.

[129] This link https://youtu.be/bV9OSlQcDhg is to a webinar on the model of the tailored method we use in the Uruk Platform.

[130] This link https://youtu.be/9hzO8O1SRSE is to a video recording of agile (or agility) in practice.

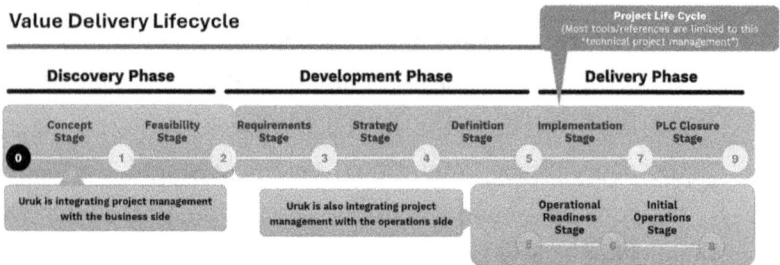

Figure No 12.2: The UrukPM Value Delivery Methodology

- In the Discovery Phase, we define the product vision[131] and business case and perform the feasibility study.
- In the Development Phase, we progressively elaborate on the product vision. We clarify the stakeholders' expectations, define business, technical, and functional requirements, develop a project management plan, define the delivery strategy, and conduct the initial design (preliminary engineering, product roadmap, product backlog, etc.). In other words, this is an iterative product and project scope development.
- Although the previous illustration does not show it, it is during the delivery phase that we use "traditional development[132]" or Agile Development.[133] Which approach to use depends on the type of product. *Refer to the following image.*

---

[131] Product Vision, Asset Vision, Venture Brief, and Project Brief are all relevant terms.

[132] We do not like the term traditional, but it is the lesser of two evils (instead of using waterfall). In Uruk, we call this the Big Bang Sequential Development approach since the final product is delivered as a big bang at the end.

[133] To ensure clarity of terms and avoid confusion about agile, we are using Iterative/Incremental Development in the Uruk Platform.

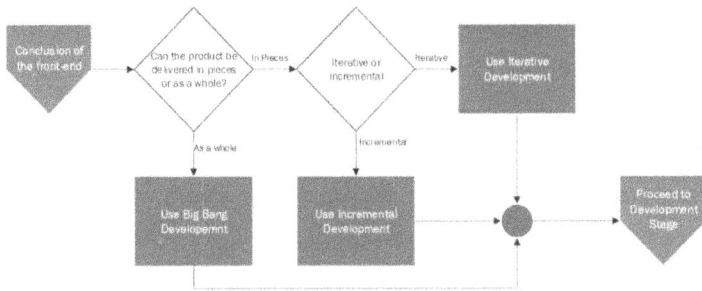

Figure No 12.3: How to Select the Development Approach?

The Importance of The Discovery Phase

One of the primary differences between Level 3 and Levels 4 and 5 is the discovery phase. We will explain its value.

Like all other phases, this phase has stages that we need to manage. In other words, we do not agree with how some project management guides classify these stages as outside the project life cycle and the project management mandate.

The organizational units' personnel managing the discovery stages might not have project management experience. Yet, they are making decisions that could be "set in stone." Therefore, they are locking a commitment that might not be readily undone later if proven deficient. Some references and project management literature call this the commitment bias (Flyvbjerg & Gardner, 2023).

Various studies have shown that the success and failure of the project are often pre-determined in this phase. The feasibility study is the primary contributor to project success or failure. Even problems encountered during the delivery phase could be attributed to the discovery phase.[134]

Remember, to predetermine success, we need a sound business case and a proper feasibility study. Without them, organizations may not be able to cultivate and achieve success.

The Importance of The Operational Stages

Another difference between Levels 3/4 and Level 5 is the operation-related stages.

Change management is one of the most crucial factors, including the operational stages in the project life cycle. We often use change management to mean:

- Project change management, i.e., a change in scope or the project's plan.
- Organizational change management focused on transforming business processes or launching new products/assets.

Let us combine the second bullet with the fact that projects are mostly change initiatives, where we create something new or implement significant changes to an existing system. Therefore, let us consider a project where we are launching a new system, a digital solution. What typically happens?

---

[134] The Uruk Platform has two deliverables in the Discovery Phase: a Project Brief that includes strategic alignment and the business case. Also, a feasibility study report with more than ten areas to evaluate, including market analysis, financial modeling, and business and market risks.

Project management is often limited to technical project management. In other words, project management only exists in the IT department and is not integrated with the business. Also, PM is not integrated with operations. There is a need for integration, what we call operational readiness, since while the development team is building the product, another team needs to get ready to accept and use the product efficiently. If these things do not happen in parallel and are not coordinated, we might end up with a completed product, but the organization is not ready to release or use it.

Another scenario is on capital projects, where the engineering and construction team completes the physical entity. Still, operations are not ready to accept or operate it if they do not start their change management early.

Therefore, integrating organizational change management and operational readiness activities into the project management process can help to ensure that projects are implemented successfully and that the organization is prepared to adopt and benefit from the project outcomes.

The Integration

Overview

How do we ensure this horizontal integration?

Why do we need this integration?

The quick answer to the second question is change management.

However, to answer the first question, we address some concepts to ensure achieving the value from this horizontal integration.

- Establish clear project objectives,
- Establish acceptance criteria and project success criteria,
- Identify all relevant stakeholders,
- Frame the opportunity through proper feasibility,
- Conduct a change impact assessment, which could also be part of the feasibility study
- Develop a change management plan,
- Develop an operational readiness plan,
- Integrate change management and operational readiness activities into the project plan,
- Monitor and evaluate progress,
- Assess project success in line with the defined criteria and
- Capture lessons learned for future enhancements.

Roles And Responsibilities

We have not discussed the human side of all the above; that is a significant discussion and is outside the scope of this work. However, we must stress that project success is collaborative among various team members. What we need is the following:

- The project sponsor (ideally from the business or sponsoring organizational unit),
- The project manager (from project management),
- An operational readiness manager (from operations, often the owner),
- The project management team (from project management),

- The rest of the project team (technical resources from various organizational units), and
- Ongoing engagements with the relevant stakeholders.

Possible Working Relations

Project sponsors, managers, and teams can take the following steps:

- Build relationships with stakeholders, especially in the areas that are traditionally outside project management scope,
- Facilitate requirements gathering workshops,
- Conduct research and analysis,
- Collaborate with cross-functional teams,
- Communicate clearly and often, with an understanding of the audience diversity,
- Have an excellent knowledge of the organization's strategic direction,
- Also, know the industry and trends affecting the industry,
- Determine if the project aligns with the strategy; if not, have the courage to stop the project.

A Visual

The following illustration *(Figure No 12.4: Integration of Project Management Across the Project Life Cycle with the Various Organizational Functions)* hides some content since a detailed discussion is outside the scope of this book.[135] However, it is essential to focus on the top two rows, which illustrate the project life cycle and the focus of each phase. The remaining rows represent the various

---

[135] This link is to a webinar recording on integrations and is related to this illustration: https://youtu.be/cDLW7C7yunc.

organizational units that should be involved in the projects. This is only to demonstrate the concept, and we must note that we could have more than five rows (lanes). The hidden part is what should be happening in every phase and stage by the various units.

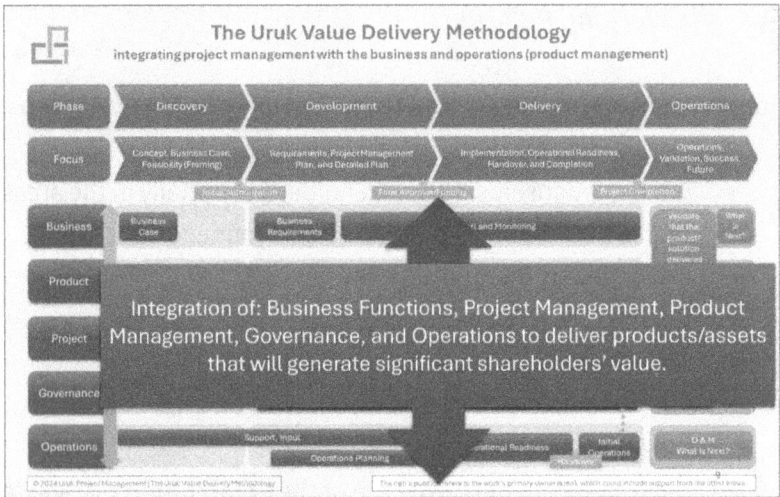

Figure No 12.4: Integration of Project Management Across the Project Life Cycle with the Various Organizational Functions

Closing Comments

The following are vital points to remember as we close this chapter.

- Organizations must have project management systems and methods,
- Ideally, the OPMS should be based on the three pillars of people (competence), processes (methods), and tools (technology),
- The methodological model must include the components of a project management method that we outlined,

- An adaptive methodology is customizable and adaptable, producing unique tailored methods,
- If your project can be successful with task management, stage management, or technical project management, that is OK,
- However, we advise project owners to use this value delivery approach, increasing their chances of success.

CHAPTER 13

Project Success

Introduction

The primary objective of this proposal is for organizations to realize their visions and purposes. This means ensuring and maximizing shareholders' value, which requires impactful strategy implementation, with project management as the strategic skill and engine for success. Therefore, organizational success partially depends on portfolio success, which requires program and project success.

Further, earlier in this book, we explained that we (the community) do not have a standard or guide to help organizations define and assess success. Often, the definition is limited to a misunderstood concept, the Triple Constraints (or Iron Triangle). Recently, there has been a push to shift the definition to value. However, the ambiguity of the definition is leading to more confusion.

Accordingly, we have developed the Four Dimensions of Project Success, mentioned earlier in the book. It is helpful to include this topic so our readers can visualize success in the envisioned future.

Gaps in Practice

Here are some of the gaps that we have observed:

- Some project management practitioners view project success from one angle, such as from the perspective of a service provider or a technical project manager, but not from the project owner's viewpoint, which is why the project exists in the first place.
- When practitioners discuss project success, it is unclear if they are discussing the success of the project management effort or the success of the project's business objectives. In other words, when they claim that 70% of projects fail (a common but unsubstantiated claim), are they talking about cost and schedule troubles or that these projects were stopped or failed to achieve their objectives?
- Furthermore, the lack of establishing project success criteria is another gap in everyday practice. During the project authorization, project and executive management should define and agree on the criteria to determine project success. Therefore, we know that some organizations ignore establishing success criteria, do not perform a proper definition of success, or do not communicate it to the project team. The threat here is that, with no criteria, how can an organization assess project success and learn for the future? If organizations cannot assess, how do they ensure proper project governance and a sound investment of the shareholders' funds?
- There is a shared view among some practitioners that all we need to assess success is to determine if the customer was satisfied or happy. This might be okay for small and simple

projects. However, it does not provide insights other than the subjective assessment. Also, it does not work on most projects, especially those that are not straightforward and have many stakeholders.

- Recently, we have seen much debate on the role of the project manager in project success and the idea that the PM should be accountable for the objective success. Although the intent behind this concept is good, it is faulty and severely deficient.[136]

Perspectives

Organizational Perspective

When dealing with success, it is necessary to take an organizational perspective. Therefore, a project's success (or failure) is for the organization and is not limited to the project manager or the project management function.

Project Owner Perspective

In line with the above, we must emphasize that we view projects from the owner's perspective. This means that organizations should not limit their views to product delivery but must go beyond that. They need to view a project as a business venture rather than an output the project team produces before demobilizing.

---

[136] A short video on this: https://youtu.be/K2d2WI2Czrk.

Visualize the following:

- Service providers' success might be limited to delivering the output within the client's requirements and realizing a profit.
- For the project management function in organizations, success might confine itself to delivering an output that complies with the specifications and is delivered on time and within budget.
- However, success is more complicated than this for the project owner (the sponsoring division), as explained through the four dimensions.

The Four Dimensions

Why the four dimensions?

Well, the primary purpose of a success model is to determine success. However, **other than this determination (good or bad), how can we learn from what happened and identify gaps for possible continual improvement?**

The four-dimensional model allows us to define and assess success at different points along the project life cycle, and each point offers a different focus. This information is an excellent source of insight for the portfolio management team to identify consistent pain points. For example, if most projects struggle with one dimension much more than the others, that will be an immediate flag. Accordingly, the organization must focus on the areas that lead to consistent problems, which would be a priority.

Please reflect on the above once you learn about the four dimensions.

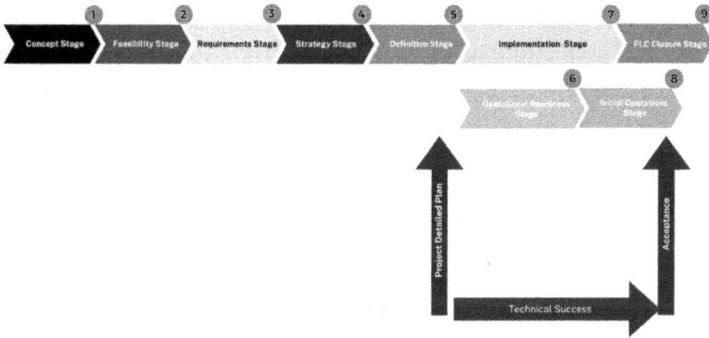

Figure No 13.1: D1, Technical Success

Technical Success

This first dimension of success assesses whether the team achieved the technical success of the product. In other words, did the team:

- Complete the work?
- Deliver the product?
- Meet the technical standards and specifications?

The following figure presents this view, highlighting the following key points:

- The client (internal or external) works with the project management team to determine the success of the delivered product.
- The team can measure this dimension with a focus on quality, scope, and specifications.

- The measurement is compared to the project's detailed plan (PDP), which is the plan used for final approval and funding in the model we present.
- Because measurement is per the PDP, this is primarily a technical assessment of the product compared to the specifications.

Project Management Success

The second illustration shows the second dimension, project management success.

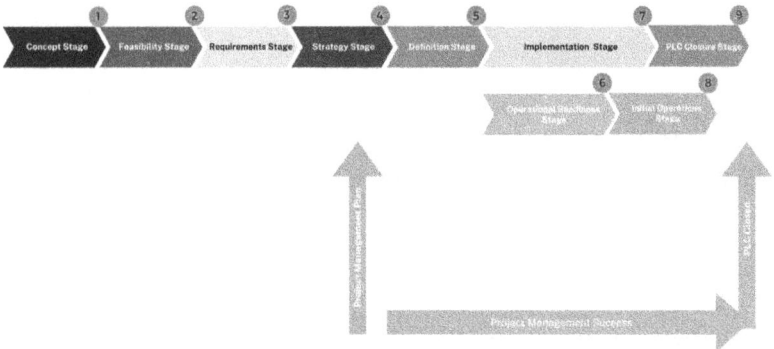

Figure No 13.2: D2, Project Management Success

This dimension assesses whether the project management team delivered the project successfully per the PM plan.

- The focus is time, cost, and other compliance requirements.
- Did the team deliver the project per the organizational project management standards?
- Did they deliver it per the established performance metrics and parameters?

- The client (internal or external) works with the project management team to determine this success criteria.
- The team measures success in this dimension compared to the PMP (project management plan).
- The team performs the success measurement during the PLC Closure Stage, with stage gate 9 (per this model).[137]

Product Delivery Success

Next, we share the illustration for the third dimension.

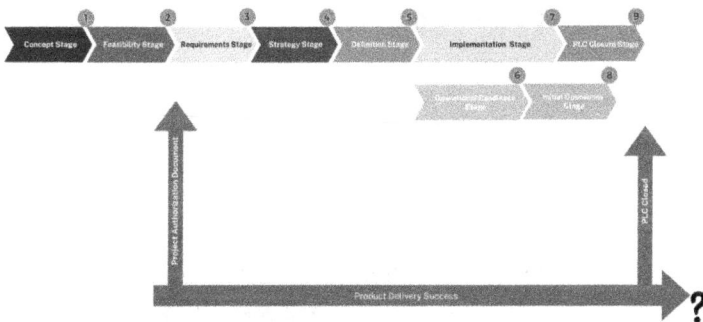

Figure No 13.3: D3, Product Delivery Success

The purpose of the third dimension is to assess whether the team did deliver the product successfully.

- Delivering product success per the project's detailed plan (PDP) (the first dimension).
- Delivering the project per the project management plan (PMP) (the second dimension).

---

[137] A reminder, we advocate the idea of tailored methods and that a project life cycle could be four or 10+ stages. Therefore, what we label as stage gate 9 here could be stage gate 4 or 10+.

- Achieving any other factor specified in the project authorization document (PAD) (the project charter).

The first two bullets above refer to the first two project success dimensions, which require input to this third dimension. Failing to deliver the product per the PDP and the PMP is a product delivery failure. If one of the dimensions is not met, we consider product delivery a failure (or at least partially).

Assuming the first two dimensions align with the criteria, the third bullet refers to other factors, which would be project—or organization-specific.

For example:

- In the case of an industrial plant, the success criteria can include customer satisfaction, achieving plant capacity within six months of final acceptance, no issues or gaps in the operating and maintenance procedures, etc.
- In an information system project, the additional criteria might be the end users' feedback and satisfaction rating.
- In a marketing project, the third dimension could include valuable feedback on the marketing campaign and customer satisfaction.

When can the team assess the project delivery success?

In some situations, evaluating this dimension at the project's close is possible, but it is not likely. For most projects, the organization might have to wait months to be confident about this dimension, represented in the "?" symbol in the figure.

The organization can measure the third dimension in comparison to the PAD.

Some practitioners might say this is not the project manager's responsibility.

We agree, especially because assessing success per this dimension might not be possible before demobilizing the team. However, the UrukPM Value Delivery Methodology (and Four Dimensions) takes the organization's perspective. It is not limited to the effectiveness of technical project management, nor is it a project manager performance assessment tool. Therefore, measuring project success is primarily an *organizational* rather than a *project manager* activity. Then, the person responsible for this dimension would be the project sponsor, who issues the PAD. Per our proposal, the project management division, the portfolio management unit, would take ownership at this point (after the project management team demobilization).

Objectives Success

The fourth and last dimension is the business[138] or objectives success, illustrated next.

---

[138] The use of the term business here is in the general context and is not specific to for-profit projects. If the project is for a not-for-profit, non-governmental organization (NGO), or government, then the driver for the project is a social or community need, not financial returns.

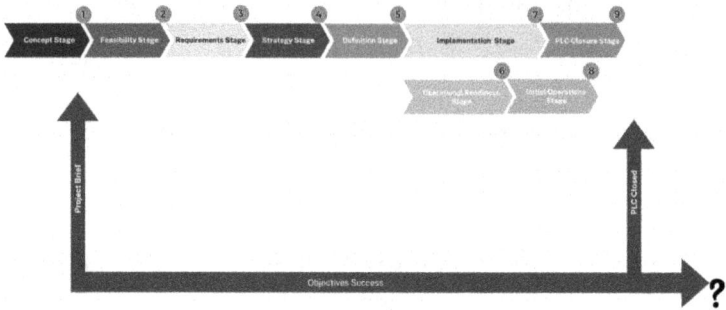

Figure No 13.4: D4, Objectives Success

This dimension is designed to assess whether the project outcome resulted in delivering the expected capabilities, which in turn led to realizing the benefits that the organization outlined at the start of the project. In other words, this dimension is linked to *realizing benefits*.

Some may argue that this is the same dimension as product delivery success. This may be the case for some projects, but not always.

Why?

The fourth dimension concerns the expected benefits and the justification behind the project. The third dimension, by contrast, concerns the PAD. The sponsor may not have developed the PAD properly to reflect the essence of the project so that the project team could deliver a good project according to the PAD. Still, from the organization's perspective, they delivered the wrong project.

Please refer to the examples used in the third dimension and reflect on them in the fourth dimension; we notice the differences.

- In the case of an industrial plant, the success criteria could be achieving a return on investment.
- In an information system project, the criteria could be reducing staff or increasing productivity.
- In a marketing project, project success would increase leads by X%.

Applying the Concept

Case Study

Let us review this real-case scenario.

A client, an organization that sells valves and pipes for the petroleum industry, wants to build a gymnasium (gym) at one of its warehouses (facility).

What is the project?

Most will say "the gym."

Is it?

Is the company in the business of building gymnasiums?

No!

OK—then what is the project?

We should ask the following question: What is the business objective of the project—*the driver?*

Oh! Now we can say: improve employee health.

Great; now it is evident.

So, how do we measure success?

- **Technical Success**. Did the team deliver the gym per the PDP? Did they deliver the building and equipment per the given standards and requirements? If yes, that is good; the first measure has been achieved.

- **Project Management Success**. Did the team deliver the gym per the PMP within the time and cost parameters? If yes, that is wonderful; another measure achieved.

- **Product Delivery Success**. Did the team deliver the gym according to the PAD? Another way to consider this is if the team delivered an acceptable and safe standard gymnasium. If yes, then excellent: The organization achieved the third measure. One can also include whether the staff liked the gym and are using it.

- **Objectives Success**. Did the project contribute to improving employee health? Proper measurement cannot occur until many months after the gym's completion.

Case Study Alternatives

Let's look at the same project from different angles.

Scenario 1

If you are a project manager, and **management mandates you to build a gymnasium**, would you think of the fourth aspect of success, improving employee health? Or would your focus be on building a gym project? Focusing on building the gym means focusing only on the facility. What do you think?

Scenario 2

Let us ask the same question with a slightly different idea statement.

Management mandates that you deliver a product to improve employee health (without mention of a gym). What will your project look like? It could include a gymnasium or not. It might include subsidized memberships to health clubs. It will likely include an awareness campaign about good health or sessions on healthy eating or cooking.

Scenario 3

In this third scenario, we will ask the same question differently.

The management mandate is to improve employee health by building a gym. This project will likely include elements from the two earlier scenarios. The project manager will focus on building the gym and conducting a health awareness campaign. With this latter scenario, the chance of success—business objective success—is much higher. In this case, the project team should include an assessment of the employees' current health so they can later use it to compare the results.

As the above shows, changing the project brief slightly—even by a few words—can make a dramatic difference to the project. Do you think achieving this project's business objective would be more likely with Scenario 3 than Scenario 1 or 2?

The PCA Model, Closing Comments

This is an excellent place to share our perspective on the PCA model[139]. PCA stands for Predetermined, Cultivated, and Achieved. It is the mindset for proactively thinking about project success.

> **PROJECTS DELIVER VALUE WHEN SUCCESS IS PREDETERMINED, CULTIVATED, AND ACHIEVED**

The Uruk Way amplifies value and drives success at every step of the value delivery life cycle, from initial vision onward. We built a methodology on the notion that project managers didn't need another tool or box to check. Instead, they require an approach to injecting an organization with foundational knowledge, allowing internal capability building and turning insight into long-term learning that contributes to future portfolio success. Understanding that philosophy is only as powerful as its ability to be applied and communicated holistically, UrukPM strives to ensure its proposal for

---

[139] A relevant video: https://youtu.be/wQrl9HvV1Xs.

an envisioned future contains tailored practices unique to the value delivery life cycle of every organization.

Predetermined

In Chapter 1, we shared the following:

Can We Predetermine Success?

Well, it depends on how you read or understand "predetermine."

Some view it as a guarantee. In that case, we cannot predetermine success since no one can guarantee it.

However, we intend to use this word to **stress the need for executives and project teams to proactively think of success consciously and consistently instead of wishing or hoping for success**. When we wish or hope for success, we might accept failure or less-than-optimal performance and settle for completion as success. **We want to change the paradigm from tolerating failure to achieving success, which starts with our intentional predetermination.**

Accordingly, predetermining success consists of three vital steps:

1. Establishing **a solid business case** for the change initiative (project or program).
2. A sound business case is insufficient. We must conduct **a proper feasibility study**. A feasibility study helps an organization decide if it can successfully deliver the change initiative and realize the expected benefits. If in doubt, the project should be stopped.

3. We decided to move forward; what is next? Could we define the success criteria? Without well-defined and quantitative (where possible) criteria, success is subjective to opinion-based assessment. The Uruk Way Four Dimensions of Project Success recommends **establishing the criteria for all four dimensions early in the project**.

Cultivated

How do we cultivate success?

Once the team predetermines what success should look like, they must maintain focus and nurture and cultivate each action along the challenging journey of a project's life. They can achieve this through a methodological process like the Value Delivery Methodology (VDM), a project life cycle/stage gate model. A competent team understands that the success of every stage is a direct contributor to the vision. Therefore, they must stay diligent in every project step to minimize risks, reduce challenges, and maximize the chance of success.

Achieved

Achieving success is a significant endeavor. Here, we remind the reader that success should not be subjective to opinion or limited to completion equal success. The team can succeed and realize the benefits with clear criteria and dedicated focus. **It is all about Vision Realized**!

CLOSING

CHAPTER 14

Final Reflections

Introduction

We invite you to revisit Chapter 1 and re-read the Executive Nightmare and the Executive Dream. While in Chapter 1, you might as well re-read the Hidden Battle section.

As you reflect on this book, remember:

Vision Realized is for organizations that can predetermine, cultivate, and achieve success.

We need executives to have a clear mindset and understand, recognize, and accept that project management is strategically important and indispensable for organizational success. Organizations should not continue treating project management as a low-level transactional or operational activity.

Now that you are in the last chapter, **we aspire that this book will lead to actions and encouragement to take the initial steps for a vital transformation.** We trust that you can envision the outcome in a few sentences:

Executives and boards of directors owe it to their shareholders to recognize and accept project management as a core organizational function indispensable for success. Despite the challenges, take a leap of faith. However, executives must hold the project management function (collectively) accountable for consistently elevating performance. Remember, it is a partnership at all levels, from formulating the strategy to generating value, one project at a time!

It Is Time For Action!

The best and most effective approach to this change initiative and the vital transformation is to follow these two most common paths:

- **Top-down:** The organizational governance authority (executives and board of directors) is responsible. This book is at the heart of this path. For project management to deliver value, we need executives' support, sponsorship, and active engagement.

- **Bottom-up:** In parallel to the top-down path, executive management must work with the project management personnel and managers to enhance their competence and improve projects' performance. In this case, they must be supported to excel while held accountable.

Our proposed solution must pursue both paths to be most effective. It is vital to understand that **this is about transformation, which takes time and requires patience, hence the need for an effective transformational team**.

Where do you start?

It depends on where you are today. We offer a few scenarios below. However, what is vital is to act NOW, regardless of where you are in your organizational journey or growth. Growth is painful but rewarding, and those aspiring for greatness realize the journey's challenges.

The scenarios

1. If your organization does not have formal, documented project management practices, we advise you to take the first step and learn. We can collaborate with you to raise awareness and strategize how to proceed along this exciting journey.

2. If your organization has already started the project management journey, you may already have a few project managers and be considering some standardization or a PMO. You can continue this path, and we advise you to refer to the PMO Continuum we shared in Chapter 5.

3. It is possible that you already have a PMO. In that case, conduct a compelling, detailed, and unbiased assessment to identify any potential gaps or inhibitors to performance. Once you do this exercise, you can determine the next steps.

4. If your organization is already doing well and has a PMO performing and contributing to success, the question is: Can you do better? Would taking the PMO to the next level, a formal project management division, enhance success? We think so, how about you?

5. In some cases, you might already have a project management division, such as those in capital projects (or service providers). In this case, is your project management division

genuinely owning the project management function across the entire organization or limiting the work to capital projects? How are they doing in marketing, human resources, or information technology?

In his book Hidden Potential, Adam Grant stresses that we do not need to aim for perfection. Instead, we must work hard toward a tomorrow that will be better than today (Grant, Hidden Potential: The Science of Achieving Greater Things, 2023).

What Are The Risks Of No Action?

Please start by going back to Chapter 2 to re-read about massive failures and successes. That will help prepare you for this next part.

Doing nothing is a choice!

Doing nothing because you are already perfect might be acceptable. However, is your organization's performance perfect? Well, maybe if you are one of the 2.5% of organizations that achieve 100% of their projects (PwC, 2014). We are confident that even those in the 2.5% group can identify opportunities for improvement, but they do not have the urgency to act!

However, reality tells us that most organizations can do better for a better future. So doing nothing out of fear and intimidation is a crippling mindset. The future is uncertain, and the level of effort can be significant or even massive. However, this is not about embarking on an impossible journey. Condensing and accelerating a massive effort in an abbreviated time leads to failure.

We suggest using program agility and slowly building one brick at a time, iteratively and incrementally. Each increment can be a short-duration effort, allowing the short-term focus and testing before moving on to the next increment.

Another approach would be to identify the most severe gaps or problems and handle those first, seeking some quick wins.

If you are not ready to go all the way, consider a PMO first and revisit the PMO Continuum to implement step by step. If you already have a PMO, how can you improve its performance and value and elevate it? In all cases, **we stress the need to go all the way and formalize the project management function through a division!**

Once Again, The Envisioned Future

As an executive, do you think there is room for improvement even in organizations doing well on projects?

What can you do if you are in an organization with frequent challenges and even project management failures? Can you sustain these challenges? Can you continue to tolerate these pain points?

What do you need to sleep better at night and enjoy your dreams while avoiding nightmares?

If you could transform the current state into a better future, would it not be pleasant to spend more leisure time with your loved ones?

How about your staff and teams? Would they enjoy being part of an organization that consistently produces success? Wouldn't this be motivational and reduce stress and turnover?

With increased competence, organizations can achieve more success; success is motivational; motivations drive more success, and success benefits all (teams, executives, and shareholders). In other words, would it not be great to grow and prosper instead of being trapped in a cycle of doom?

Can you and your organization transform and become a beacon of light shining on the road to a fantastic future?

Closing Remarks

We encourage you to have the courage to explore and travel the rugged roads to reach the beauty of nature and life. We aspire to have you join those of us with the will and determination to break the status quo and aspire for a better future!

In conclusion, project management is a cornerstone of competitive advantage, driving organizational success in today's dynamic business landscape. Organizations can achieve their strategic goals precisely and efficiently by meticulously planning, executing, and monitoring projects and programs. Project management's value lies in its ability to deliver projects within the time and budget parameters and its capacity to foster innovation, enhance team collaboration, and mitigate risks. As we navigate an era of rapid change and complexity, the indispensable role of project management becomes ever more evident, ensuring that organizations remain flexible, resilient, consistent, and poised for sustained success.

Realizing the Vision

Some References

1. **Website**: The UrukPM Website has a knowledge-sharing section with links to various sites and includes case studies, professional papers, and other resources: https://urukpm.com/project-management-resources/.

2. **Audio Channel**: We have a podcast, The 4PMs Podcast, which you can find on most platforms. Here is a link to our website: https://urukpm.com/project-management-podcast/.

3. **Video Channel**: UrukPM hosts the Applied Project Management Channel: https://www.youtube.com/@urukprojectmanagement.

4. **Blog Site**: UrukPM also offers the Applied Project Management blog, https://urukpm.com/blog/.

Additional Resources

1. **E-Books**: We have published numerous e-books, which you can find on the Bookboon.com website. Here is a link: https://bookboon.com/en/mounir-a-ajam-author.

2. **Books**: Our other books were published in print and include e-book versions. You can find those on Amazon, Barnes & Noble, and other book vendors. Search for **Mounir A. Ajam** as the author.

3. **A Special Website Page**: The following link, https://urukpm.com/transforming-project-management/, leads to a website page dedicated to **Transforming Project Management**, including a video and other relevant collaterals. In the video, we explain our views on the need for transformation with the trilogy of books in progress. You already have the first one in your hands.

4. **LinkedIn Group**: We have also created a LinkedIn Group focusing on Transforming Project Management, https://www.linkedin.com/groups/14315058/. You are welcome to join it.

Starting the Journey

We are excited that you have acquired this book and read it. We realize there are many things to consider and unpack. You do not have to do it alone; we are here for you. **Why not schedule a strategy session today to discuss the possibility and envision a bright future where vision is realized**: https://calendly.com/mounirajam/?

BACK MATTER

Bibliography

Ajam, M. A. (2017). *Project Management Beyond Waterfall and Agile.* CRC Press.

Ajam, M. A. (2020). *Leading Megaprojects, A Tailored Approach.* CRC Press.

Ajam, M. A. (2023). Transforming the project management state of practice. *University of Texas Dallas: Project Management Symposium*, (p. 15). Dallas.

Ajam, M. A. (2024). Strategic Program Management, The Uruk Case Study. *University of Texas Dallas: Project Management Symposium*, (p. 18). Dallas.

Barshop, P. (2016). *Capital Projects.* Wiley.

Buiness Process Management Office, Process Maturity. (n.d.). Retrieved December 2024, from University of California Berkeley: https://bpm.berkeley.edu/process-architecture/process-maturity

CII Best Practices. (n.d.). Retrieved from Construction Industry Institute: https://www.construction-institute.org/cii-best-practices

Favaro, K. (2015, March 31). *Defining Strategy, Implementation, and Execution*. Retrieved 2024, from Harvard Business Review: https://hbr.org/2015/03/defining-strategy-implementation-and-execution

Flyvbjerg, B., & Gardner, D. (2023). *How Big Things Get Done*. Pan Macmillan.

Grant, A. (2021). *Think Again: The Power of Knowing What You Don't Know*. Viking.

Grant, A. (2023). *Hidden Potential: The Science of Achieving Greater Things*. Viking.

Ibbs, C., & Reginato, J. (2002). *Quantifying the Value of Project Management*. Project Management Institute (PMI).

IT difficulties help take Kmart down. (2002, January 28). Retrieved 2024, from Computer World: https://www.computerworld.com/article/1351181/it-difficulties-help-take-kmart-down.html

Lerner, M. (2020, October 21). *Government Tech Projects Fail by Default*. Retrieved 2024, from Belfer Center (Harvard Kennedy School): https://www.belfercenter.org/publication/government-tech-projects-fail-default-it-doesnt-have-be-way

Manifesto for Agile Software Development. (n.d.). Retrieved from agilemanifesto.org: https://agilemanifesto.org/

Merrow, E. W. (2011). *Industrial Megaprojects: Concepts, Strategies, and Practices for Success*. Wiley.

Pfeffer, J., & Sutton, R. I. (1999). *The Knowing-Doing Gap.* Harvard Business Review Press.

PwC. (2014). *Project Management: Improving Perfromance, Reducing Risk.*

Saalmuller, L. (2022, November 17). Retrieved 2024, from Harvard Business School Onlie: https://online.hbs.edu/blog/post/strategy-formulation-and-implementation

Schoper, Y.-G., Wald, A., Ingason, H., & Fridgeirsson, T. (2018, January). Projectification in Western economies: A comparative study of Germany, Norway and Iceland. *International Journal of Project Management*, 71-82. Retrieved 2024, from Science Direct: https://www.sciencedirect.com/science/article/abs/pii/S0263786317306348?via%3Dihub

Stage Gate International. (n.d.). Retrieved 2024, from Stage Gate International: https://www.stage-gate.com/

Why a botched IT Project will destroy a major corporation in the near future. (2013, April 8). Retrieved 2024, from Technology Review.

About the Author

Mounir A. Ajam is a distinguished project management expert, author, advisor, and speaker. He is the **Founder and CEO of Uruk Project Management**.

Mounir is a senior executive with **over three decades of outstanding global and practical experience** in the capital projects industries, such as engineering, construction, petroleum, utilities, project management, and management consulting. He has worked on projects worth billions of United States dollars in North America, Europe, Southeast Asia, and West Asia. His experience includes working on small/multiple projects and large and complex projects, including mega projects in the United States and Southeast Asia. His experience includes management consultancy and training for leading organizations from East Africa to Southeast Asia. Most recently, Mounir has been leading a technology startup developing project management software solutions. **He is the innovator behind the comprehensive, versatile, and integrated digital solution, the Uruk Platform.**

He is the author of several books, including *Project Management Beyond Waterfall and Agile* and *Leading Megaprojects, A Tailored Approach*. **His work focuses on advancing project management**

methodologies and practices. He is known for his innovative, Customizable, and Adaptable Methodology for Managing Projects (CAMMP™), now rebranded as **the UrukPM Value Delivery Methodology** and the **Four Dimensions of Project Success.**

In addition to his professional achievements, Mounir is deeply committed to community development and volunteer work. He actively supports various global project management organizations and initiatives, contributing his expertise to help build and sustain project management functions in different sectors. Most recently, he was part of the team reviewing PMI's PMO Guide, which will be published in 2025.

Finally, Mounir often shares his knowledge through publishing blog articles, podcasts, videos, webinars, and workshops. He has also presented professional papers by speaking at project management conferences worldwide.

About UrukPM

Uruk Project Management (UrukPM) is a specialized technology-enabled management consultancy founded by Mounir A. Ajam. We are a tech startup.

The company is dedicated to transforming how organizations lead projects by integrating project management with product and asset management.

Uruk Project Management aims to help organizations elevate performance, optimize capital deployment, and maximize shareholder and stakeholder value. Their innovative approach, the Uruk Way Project Management Framework, emphasizes collaboration and integration across various business units and operations. Further, UrukPM is the company leading the development of the Uruk Platform, a Software as a Service (SaaS) solution.

The company aims to help organizations bridge the gap between vision and achievement by providing comprehensive, integrated project management solutions. Uruk Project Management is committed to sustainability, diversity, and inclusion, ensuring its practices benefit its clients and uplift society. With a focus on innovation and accountability, Uruk Project Management strives to be a leading solution provider and advocate for global project management excellence.

The Uruk Way

The Uruk Way is the short version of the Uruk Way Project Management Framework, https://urukpm.com/the-uruk-way-project-management/. We use the label for the UrukPM Project Management Innovation Program, which we started in our earlier company, SUKAD, in 2007. An alternative term is The Uruk Framework.

The Uruk Way stands for our contribution to the global project management community. UrukPM plays a role in creating and disseminating knowledge through this project management innovation program. Currently, the Uruk Way products include the following:

1. The Value Delivery Methodology, previously the Customizable and Adaptable Methodology for Managing Projects (CAMMP),
2. The Seven Elements of Project Management Maturity,
3. The Four Dimensions of Project Success,
4. The Four Control Reference Points, and
5. The Six Steps of Performance Management.

The above work led to many workshops, videos, blog articles, e-books, and books.

The Uruk Platform

The Uruk Platform is a comprehensive and versatile cloud-based project management solution that facilitates end-to-end product delivery processes. It is built on the principles adopted by UrukPM, which we covered in this book under the chapters on **Integrations to Deliver Value** and the **Value Delivery Methodology**. Therefore, it combines the horizontal and vertical integrations presented. It includes built-in processes (parts of the organizational project management system). Furthermore, it has extensive guides and a knowledge portal to help enhance the competence of our client's personnel.

The Uruk Platform knowledge foundation is built on decades of expertise and real-world experience in project management, integrating innovative computing technology with methodological approaches. The platform emphasizes collaboration among various business units, operations, and project management stakeholders, aiming to streamline project execution from concept formation through feasibility, definition, implementation, operations, and up to project closure and realizing the benefits.

The Uruk Platform uses the value delivery methodology. However, we subscribe to respecting the diversity of project management practice. Therefore, the methodological process allows the creation of tailored methods fit for purpose for the various contexts of industries and project types, sizes, and complexity.

The history of the Uruk Platform is rooted in the vision of Mounir A. Ajam, the founder of SUKAD Corp (now UrukPM), who sought to create a scalable and adaptable project management framework. The platform was developed to address the high failure rates in project management across various sectors by providing a centralized medium for managing projects, programs, and portfolios. It integrates project management with program, product, and portfolio management, transforming how organizations lead projects and achieve their goals.

The value of the Uruk Platform lies in its ability to enhance organizational performance significantly. Organizations using the platform can increase the speed to market, increase their chances of achieving cost and schedule objectives, and reduce the cost of leading their portfolios. The Uruk Platform helps organizations achieve higher profitability and operational excellence by fostering a culture of collaboration and informed decision-making throughout the value delivery life cycle.

The Uruk Platform is NOT a software tool. It is an innovative solution.